C000253117

THE
SMOKED FOOD
COOKBOOK

THE SMOKED FOOD COOKBOOK

Revolutionary Recipes for Smoking and Barbecue Cooking

Paul Kirk

APPLE

A QUINTET BOOK

Published by Apple Press
6 Blundell Street
London N7 9BH

Copyright © 2001 Quintet Publishing
Limited. All rights reserved. No part of this
publication may be reproduced, stored in a
retrieval system or transmitted in any form or
by any means, electronic, mechanical,
photocopying, recording or otherwise, without
the permission of the copyright owner.

ISBN 1 84092 3105

This book was conceived, designed and
produced by
Quintet Publishing Limited
6 Blundell Street
London N7 9BH

Senior Project Editor: Toria Leitch
Editor: Anna Bennett
Designer: Isobel Gillan
Photographer: Ian Garlick
Food Stylist: Kathryn Hawkins

Creative Director: Richard Dewing

Typeset in Great Britain by Central Southern
Typesetters, Eastbourne
Manufactured in Hong Kong by Regent
Publishing Services Limited
Printed in China by Midas Printing Limited

CONTENTS

Introduction

SMOKING IS enjoying a revival all over the world. With this book you will be able to learn the principles governing it and join in the fun. Try your hand at stove-top smoking or smoke your own bacon or a whole salmon. You may even be inspired to build an old-fashioned walk-in smokehouse. As you gain confidence, you will be able to experiment with different flavours and devise your own recipes, creating rubs and marinades using your favourite combination of herbs and spices.

Smoking is essentially a means of preserving meat or fish by exposing it to the aromatic smoke of burning hardwood, usually after pickling in salt or brine. Why smoke foods? Historically, smoking came about through necessity. With no refrigeration or canning procedures yet developed, people found brining and curing an effective means of preserving their food. We can safely speculate that the process came about by happy accident, when a cave man concealed some meat on a ledge above the fire he burned to cook on and forgot about it for some days or weeks. When he or someone else eventually came upon it they found it to be dry and smoked and not rotten.

Historical references to smoke-cooking abound. There is a barbecue or smoking pit in central China, for example, which is reported to be more than 5000 years old. Sausages, which the Romans referred to as *salus*,

Left Seasoning your food before smoking helps to give it a really distinctive flavour.

Below A simple salad or grilled vegetables are the perfect accompaniment to a spicy smoked chicken dish.

Right *The author, Paul Kirk (far left) and his team prepare for a cooking session.*

meaning salted or preserved, are mentioned in Babylonian records dating from 1500 B.C. and Homer refers to blood sausage in 900 B.C. A Cypriot text dating from the fifth century B.C. refers to salami, and the Italian method of cooking in wood fired ovens is well documented in history. To this day a great delicacy in Iceland is smoked lamb, which is cured then buried in the ground to mature. In South Africa they still produce sun-dried meat called biltong, and in many countries dried salt cod is used as a base for many interesting and traditional dishes. As methods have become more refined, hot-smoking has progressed to smoke-roasting and nowadays there are all manner of smokers and techniques to choose from when cooking your food in this way.

The primary function of brines nowadays is to enhance the flavour of meat or fish rather than preserve it. With an increasingly varied store of ingredients now available to us world-wide, and global influences in cooking and flavouring, the opportunity to create revolutionary smoking sensations is too good to miss. The examples of brining and curing included in this book are not the traditional brines. These were more concerned with preserving than flavouring, and were often a hit-and-miss business because people kept no records of how they had made the brine and were not too specific about quantities.

Enrich your culinary repertoire by exploring this exciting area of cooking and remember that it is not as difficult as it might sound. Smoke-cooking is essentially a simple art that relies on good-quality ingredients to produce a delicious result. Have fun and enjoy!

Smoking Know-how

SMOKE-COOKING is not as complicated as it sounds. Start with the best ingredients you can find so that you get great results every time. Have patience and document what you do, step by step. This is not as laborious as it might seem. Finally, enjoy what you are doing and have fun.

When I was first introduced to the world of smoking it was twofold – part preserving and part flavouring. Today it is mostly done for flavour. The recipes in this cookbook are for flavour and enjoyment, not preserving. Even the bacon recipe needs to be refrigerated after curing and smoking. Smoke helps to preserve food, but it is primarily used to enhance the flavour of the food.

Smoke is usually generated by a heat source, charcoal, gas, electricity or wood. In smoke-cooking the smoky flavour comes from hardwoods, each of which produces a slightly different flavour. Hickory is one of the most popular. Some of the other woods you can choose from are apple, cherry, oak, maple, alder, nut and aged fruitwoods; peach, plum, pear and orange also work well. Usually the hardwood that is indigenous to your area is your best bet to start with. Green wood burns at a higher temperature and for a longer time than aged wood (that is, wood that has been cut and dried for at least 6 months). It also provides more smoke.

Left *Turning the meat during cooking is important to help distribute the smoked flavour evenly.*

Below *The results speak for themselves with this spicy chilli-rubbed rack of lamb (see page 68).*

COOKING-WOOD CHART

WOOD TYPE	CHARACTERISTICS	USE WITH
Acacia	Mesquite family/strong	Most meat, vegetables
Alder	Delicate with a hint of sweetness	Fish, pork, poultry, game birds and salmon
Almond	Nutty and sweet smoke flavour, light ash	Good for all meat
Apple	Slightly sweet but dense, fruity smoke flavour	Beef, poultry, game birds, pork and ham
Apricot	Milder and sweeter flavour than hickory	Good for most meat
Ash	Fast-burning, light but distinctive flavour	Good for fish and red meat
Birch	Medium-hard wood with a flavour similar to maple	Good for pork and poultry
Cherry	Slightly sweet, fruity smoke flavour	Good for all meat
Cottonwood	Very subtle flavour	Good for most meat
Grape Vines	Aromatic, similar to fruitwoods	Good for all meat
Grapefruit	Medium smoke flavour with a hint of fruit	Excellent for beef, pork and poultry
Hickory	Pungent, smoky, bacon-like flavour.	Good for all smoking especially pork and ribs
Lemon	Medium smoke flavour with a hint of fruit	Excellent for beef, pork and poultry
Lilac	Very light, subtle with a floral hint	Good for seafood and lamb
Maple	Mild, smoky, somewhat sweet flavour	Good for pork, poultry, cheese, vegetables and small game birds
Mesquite	Strong earthy flavour	Most meat, especially beef and most vegetables
Mulberry	Sweet apple-like aroma	Beef, poultry, game birds, pork and ham
Nectarine	Milder and sweeter flavour than hickory	Good for most meat

WOOD TYPE	CHARACTERISTICS	USE WITH
Oak	Heavy smoke flavour. Red oak is considered the best by many pitmasters	Good for red meat, pork, fish and game
Orange	Medium smoke flavour with a hint of fruit	Excellent for beef, pork and poultry
Peach	Slightly sweet flavour	Good for most meat
Pear	Slightly sweet flavour	Poultry, game birds and pork
Pecan	More like oak than hickory, but not as strong	Good for most meat
Plum	Milder and sweeter than hickory	Good for most meat
Walnut	Very heavy smoke flavour, usually mixed with lighter wood like pecan or apple. Can be bitter if used alone or not aged	Good for red meat and game

EQUIPMENT

You don't have to spend a lot of money if you don't want to. You can make a smoker out of any barbecue grill or pit that has a cover or lid so long as you can control the temperature.

You need to be able to control the airflow to the heat source if it is charcoal, wood or a free-burning combustible product. Gas and electricity are usually controlled by means of valves and switches. Control is the ability to adjust the air supply going in (if fire has no oxygen it can't burn) as well as the air escaping, venting or exhausting. The exhaust control is where you regulate how much smoke will be kept in the food chamber. Restricting or increasing the airflow controls the burning of the charcoal and hardwood.

You should use the wood or smouldering agent in conjunction with your heat source. A smouldering agent could be wood, fresh or dried herbs, rice, tea or sugar (all three are used in the Tea-smoked duck recipe, page 39).

The smoking (food) chamber is where you place anything you want to smoke. It is usually located between the smoke generator and the exhaust.

A standard kettle barbecue is an easy way to cook smoked food when you are just starting out.

The list of cookers or smokers I have cooked on is long and varied, and includes several home-made models.

A gas grill can be used as a smoker if it has dual burners or controls.

Water smokers are usually powered by electricity or charcoal and have a domed lid, food grates, a pan for holding water and a heat source on the base. They are great for cooking foods that benefit from added moisture.

Free-standing smokehouses are another option, whether home-made or commercial. The latter range from those that will accommodate 4 large rolling racks with 5 or more smoking chambers. Catering

Below This large free-standing smoker is for serious smokers who enjoy a good cook-up.

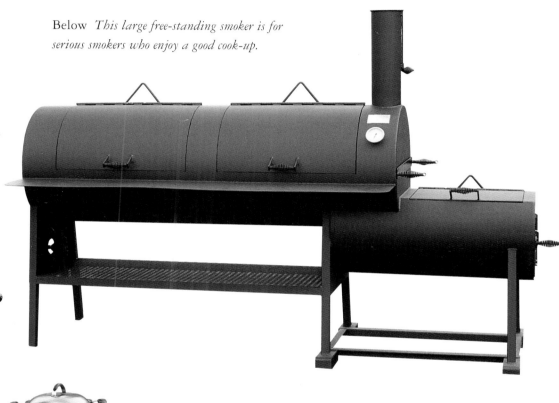

Above *The Smoky Mountain Smoker is a compact portable cooker which is large enough to accommodate a sizeable chicken or rack of ribs.*

smoking units are extremely expensive but enable you to control the heat, smoke and humidity with absolute stability.

Setting up a small cooker to be an indirect cooker or smoker is easy. Bank your charcoal briquettes to one side, (the manufacturer will tell you to bank coals on both sides of the cooker and use a water pan). What and how long you are cooking will determine the amount of charcoal you will need to use. Count how many briquettes you start with for a particular dish, keep track of the number and make a note of it for future reference. Light the charcoal, following the manufacturer's instructions. Avoid petro-chemicals if at all possible.

This gas grill can be used to smoke food and will be sufficient to feed a small party or family gathering.

Hot-smoking and Stove-top Smoking Techniques

HOT-SMOKING is a more traditional technique, not as widely practised as it used to be, most having moved on to smoke-roasting or barbecuing, which is done at a higher temperature. When I am going to hot-smoke, I pick something young, tender and succulent that will cook in 4 to 5 hours or less. You can hot-smoke for as long as you wish but I prefer to keep to this time. You must take care to keep the meat moist by using a baste, which can be a reserved marinade, a concoction of your devising or just apple juice. Melted butter makes a good baste and it is one of the best flavour enhancers you can use. I start basting halfway through the cooking process. Turn your piece of meat at this time, then baste. Repeat the basting process after a further hour and at regular intervals thereafter, as the recipe dictates. Avoid opening the smoker during the cooking time to check how the meat is doing. When you open up the smoker you can lose precious heat, smoke and temperature. Only open your smoker to turn the meat, baste or put something else on the smoker.

Stove-top smoking is good if you want a light smoke flavour and are cooking for a short time. If you are using a stove-top smoking kit, sprinkle 125 to 225 g/4 to 8 oz of sawdust in the bottom of a flameproof casserole. Place a rack over the sawdust. Place the casserole on a burner over high heat. When the sawdust starts to smoulder, place a salmon on the rack, cover with the lid and reduce the heat to medium. Cook for 20 to 30 minutes or until the fish flakes easily. Don't open the casserole before the 20 minutes. Keeping a log can be really helpful: you can develop your own stove-top smoking times and temperature charts. I have done boneless, skinless chicken breasts, using the timing above. For a whole chicken, I smoke it on the stove-top casserole until the sawdust stops smoking. Then place the chicken in a pre-heated oven and cook at 175°C/350°F/Gas Mark 4 for about 45 minutes, until it is cooked and has a pleasantly smoked flavour.

Commercial stainless-steel stove-top smokers, consisting of a 38 × 38 × 9-centimetre/15 × 11 × 3¼-inch cooking dish with a wire rack and a slide-on lid, are used in the same way as casserole stove-top smokers. You could also use a grill pan with a wire rack to keep the meat or vegetables above the sawdust or wood chips. Cover with heavy-duty aluminium foil. If the pan and rack are not deep enough to make a domed X-shaped 'tent', use spring-type wire, bending it between the opposite corners.

Above *Flavoured marinades can be used to baste the meat during cooking as well as to impart flavour before.*

Right *Hot smoking can be done on a conventional kettle barbecue in the backyard, so get your coals heated and get smokin!*

Smoke-roasting Techniques

SMOKE-ROASTING, or barbecuing, is becoming increasingly popular all over the world. All smoking – cold- and hot-smoking, smoke-roasting or barbecuing is done by indirect cooking. The fire is away from the meat or fish. Barbecuing is generally defined as slow-cooking meat with or over the heat of hardwood and/or charcoal at a temperature of 93 to 190°C/200 to 375°F.

The first thing to do before smoke-roasting is to set up the smoker. The most readily available is the kettle type, with a lid. Have a thermometer on hand, a sugar/deep-frying one is ideal, calibrated from 10 to 232°C/50 to 450°F. To test your thermometer for accuracy, place it in boiling water: it should read 100°C/212°F. You also need a cork; I like to use a champagne cork. Drill a hole in the cork about the same size as the barrel of the thermometer. Insert the thermometer barrel through the hole in the cork and it will cradle in the vent hole of the smoker lid, without the barrel touching the lid itself, enabling you to get a true temperature reading.

I prefer lump or natural charcoal to charcoal briquettes, but beginners

Below *Use the air vent to control the heat.*

Above *This pork tenderloin (see page 59) has been spiced with chillies and ginger for a real flavour kick.*

Above right *Be careful when turning fish that is nearly cooked as it can come apart; use a large spatula or fish slice.*

generally find briquettes easier to start with because they burn more evenly than natural lump charcoal. Avoid petroleum products, as these will taint the taste. You also need wood chunks or chips for flavour (see page 9).

I also suggest a water tin, which helps to retain moisture in your cooker at all times, but some people prefer not to use one. The object is to provide humidity in your smoker for the meat you are smoking. To achieve this, you can use a water tin, and baste with apple juice or cider, or dispense with the water tin and baste with a basting sauce. I use an old bread tin but you can use any tin that will work for you, bearing in mind it should be large enough so you don't have to refill it every hour. The water tin does not necessarily have to be filled with water, but using wine, beer, apple juice, cider or vinegar seems to make little or no difference to the flavour of the smoked meat.

Manufacturers usually recommend placing a water tin in the middle of the grill and charcoal fires on either side. In my opinion this restricts your cooking area. I put the fire on one side and the water tin on the other. This gives you the other three-quarters of the grill/smoker to work on. If you're cooking, you might as well fill the grill up; smoked meat freezes well.

Place your hot coals over an air vent if possible. This gives you better control of the heat by controlling the airflow. Place the water tin right up against the hot coals. Place the meat grill on the smoker, making sure that the handle-holes are directly over the hot coals. If you have a grill with flip-up grates that open on one or both sides then position them over the hot coals. Place the cover on the smoker with the vent holes opposite the hot coals. If you are smoking for more than 40 minutes to 1 hour replenish the cooker with hot coals and wood chunks as follows: place your thermometer in the vent holes. When the smoker temperature reaches 110 to 121°C/230 to 250°F or your desired cooking temperature, drop 2 wood chunks of your choice on the hot coals then place the meat on the smoker. Replace the cover on the smoker and do not open it until it is time to turn or baste the meat.

If you are planning to smoke/cook for several hours you will need to add hot coals to maintain an even temperature. As a general rule the temperature will start to drop between 40 and 60 minutes. Preheat the coals in a metal container for 20 to 30 minutes and add them to the smoker using tongs. If you keep a note of all your smoking procedures as you complete them, you will know when to start some more coals in order to get them hot. I usually start with 40 to 50 briquettes. Cut that number in half when preparing hot coals to add to the smoker – this is enough to keep the smoker at temperature for another 40 to 60 minutes. Repeat the process for as long as you're cooking.

If you are using a water smoker you can fill the charcoal ring with charcoal. Preheat some charcoal, pour the hot coals on top of the raw charcoal, add a couple of chunks of hardwood and cover it, then bring it up to temperature by adjusting the air intake and the exhaust vent. This smoker is now set up to smoke for 10 to 12 hours. Replenish the water in the water tin, turn your meat, and baste. If you are cooking with charcoal and wood you will get a smoke flavour. You can soak your wood and wood chips in water. This will give you more smoke and the fire will burn a little slower.

Below left Smoking adds a really unique and strong flavour to many varieties of fish.

Below Smoke-roasting need not be restricted to meat-eaters – vegetables respond equally well to this method of cooking.

Seasoning Techniques

CURING

Meat and fish have been cured for many centuries using salt and smoke. In time the use of saltpetre (KNO^3, potassium nitrite), became popular, but this has now been replaced with sodium nitrite, sodium nitrate, and other compounds such as absorbic acid. Chemical compounds like absorbic acid are substances that are used primarily to preserve the colour of the meat.

Much folklore surrounds the art of curing food, superstitions including the ancient belief that curing during the week of a full moon would ensure a better product that would be protected from all the elements. Procedures for curing range from packing the meat in salt and allowing it to cure for a suitable length of time. The meat was then placed or arranged on a wooden shelf or packed in a wooden box or barrel and stored in a cool, dark place, usually a cellar.

When my uncles Len and Chuck Le Cluyse cured pork bellies (bacon), usually 4 or 5 at a time, they would use about 3.6 kg/8 lb of non-iodized sea salt for every 45 kg/100 lb of meat. They would mix the salt with 900 ml to 1.1 l/1½ to 2 pt molasses (225 ml/8 fl oz per belly); 50 g/2 oz of medium

Below Mops and dry spice rubs moisten and flavor the ingredients before and during the cooking process.

Bottom right The lime juice used in the marinade for this chicken dish is enhanced by a squeeze of fresh lime when you come to serve it.

ground black pepper, and 50 g/2 oz of cayenne. They smeared the mixture all over the bellies and placed the bellies in a special wooden chest they built just for the bacon. They would then weight the chest and put it in a large refrigerator where it would cure for 6 to 8 weeks. After this time they washed the cure off the bellies and hung them in their walk-in smokehouse. They would smoke it for 3 to 6 days at about 37 to 48°C/100 to 120°F. When I cure bacon I buy one belly weighing about 8.1 to 9.9 kg/18 to 22 lb. I cut it in half and square it up. I rub it with a brown sugar cure and place it in an oak box or a plastic container. Curing your own bacon is fun, and yields a much better product than you can buy commercially.

BRINING

In times gone by, brining meant dissolving salt in water until the solution would float a raw egg. The brine would usually be heated to get more salt into the solution, then left to cool. This brine would work well with turkey and salmon. Immerse the bird or fish in the solution and weight it down with a plate and a brick, keeping it under the top of the brine. Place it in the refrigerator for 4 to 6 days. Wash the brine from the meat and smoke it.

RUBS OR BARBECUE SEASONINGS

A barbecue seasoning or rub is a dry marinade. Season the meat and put it on the cooker or leave it to marinate for 2, 4 or 6 hours or overnight in the refrigerator. Dry rubs are my choice of seasoning for most of the hot, stove-top, smoke-roasting and barbecue recipes I prepare. When making a rub I suggest equal parts of sugar and salt, (225 g/8 oz of each). I prefer granulated white sugar to brown sugar, because the moisture in the brown sugar makes

Above *Ginger, cinnamon, peppercorns, garlic, lemon, and turmeric are just some of the seasonings you can use to flavour your smoked food.*

SEASONING CHART

TIMES IN HOURS

6 to 8 Spare ribs	Venison Duck			
5 to 7	Beef roast	Beef brisket	Beef ribs	
4 to 6	Beef kebabs	Beef steaks	Lamb kebabs	Game birds
4 to overnight	Turkey	Turkey quarters	Flank steak	Skirt steak
3 to 4	Pork tenderloin	Pork chops	Pork loin	
2 to 4	Chicken breasts	Chicken	Chicken portions	Chicken wings
½ to 2	Fish	Shellfish		

it tend to clump. For salt I prefer seasoned salt, garlic salt, celery salt and onion salt. Next, I add some paprika for colour, and equal parts of chilli powder and black pepper; this recipe will handle 2 tablespoons of each. That is a basic barbecue rub. Now add your signature; pick three of your favourite spices or herbs you think will enhance the flavour of the meat you are about to smoke. If you can't decide, start with 1 teaspoon allspice, 1 teaspoon ground ginger, and ¼ teaspoon ground cloves. If you like a little kick, add 1 teaspoon cayenne as well. To apply the rub sprinkle it on like salt and pepper rather than rubbing it into the meat or fish.

MARINADES

A marinade is a liquid mixture (usually a combination of an acid ingredient such as vinegar or lemon juice, oil and seasonings) used to season meat or vegetables before cooking. The primary function of marinades is to flavour, moisten and soften rather than to tenderize, as is commonly believed. If meat is left in a marinade too long it can make the outer muscle soft and mushy. On fish and boneless, skinless chicken breast, the acid can cook the flesh.

Below *Flavouring oils with herbs, chillies and garlic will add an extra dimension to your marinade.*

SEASONING RECIPES

SEASONING, IN MY opinion, is the most important chapter in this book. The more you know about seasonings, spices and herbs the better cook you will be. I consider seasoning to be at the heart of smoked food cooking, so read through these recipes and make the best seasonings ever.

CAJUN SEASONING

Yield about 80 g/3 oz

6 Tbsp paprika
2 Tbsp garlic powder
1½ Tbsp cayenne
2 tsp dry mustard
2 tsp ground oregano
2 tsp seasoned salt
1 tsp ground thyme
1 tsp finely ground black pepper
1 tsp toasted ground cumin
1 tsp white pepper
½ tsp ground marjoram
½ tsp ground nutmeg

Combine the paprika, garlic, cayenne, mustard, oregano, seasoned salt, thyme, black pepper, cumin, white pepper, marjoram and nutmeg in a sieve over a bowl and sift. Blend well. Store the seasoning in an airtight container in a cool dry place.

CARIBBEAN CHICKEN RUB

Yield about 125 g/4 oz

3 Tbsp muscovado sugar
3 Tbsp coarse salt
1 Tbsp coarsely ground black pepper
1 Tbsp grated lemon rind
1 Tbsp grated orange rind
1 Tbsp ground allspice
1 Tbsp garlic powder
1 Tbsp onion powder
1 Tbsp ground coriander
2 tsp ground ginger

Combine the sugar, salt, black pepper, lemon rind, orange rind, allspice, garlic, onion, coriander and ginger in a bowl and blend well. Store in an airtight container in a cool dry place.

BARBECUE RUB FOR BEEF BRISKET

Yield about 275 g/10 oz

50 g/2 oz brown sugar
50 g/2 oz granulated sugar
50 g/2 oz barbecue spice
50 g/2 oz paprika
3 Tbsp celery salt
2 Tbsp salt
2 tsp black pepper
2 tsp celery seeds
1 tsp garlic powder
1 tsp cayenne

Combine the brown sugar, granulated sugar, barbecue spice, paprika, celery salt, salt, pepper, celery seeds, garlic powder and cayenne in a bowl and blend well. Store in an airtight container in a cool dry place.

SMOKED PASTRAMI

Yield about 2.7 kg to 3.6 kg/6 to 8 lb

1.8 l/3¼ pt ice-cold water
50 g/2 oz mixed sodium nitrite (or dextrose) and non-iodized salt (available in health food stores or chemists), mixed 1:16
1 Tbsp garlic juice
100 g/3½ oz sea salt
25 g/1 oz dextrose powder
One 4.5-kg/10-lb lean brisket, trimmed
225 g/8 oz coarsely ground black pepper
125 g/4 oz ground coriander
125 g/4 oz dark brown sugar (optional)

Combine the water, sodium nitrite and non-iodized salt mixture, garlic, salt and dextrose powder in a bowl, stirring with a wire whisk to dissolve the seasonings.

Using a kitchen syringe if you have one, fill it with the cure and pump generously onto the roast all over (or apply with a basting brush). Place the roast in a non-reactive container (a plastic one with a snap-on lid will work well), pour any excess cure over the roast and keep submerged in the refrigerator for 3 to 5 days.

Combine the pepper, coriander, and sugar in a small bowl and blend well. Remove the roast from the cure and rub all sides with the pepper mixture, pressing it into the meat.

Place in a smoker preheated to 82°C/180°F with the dampers open. Cook for about 1 hour until the surface of the meat is dry. Close the dampers, about one-third, add smoking wood to the heat source and smoke at this temperature for 2 hours. Gradually increase the temperature to between 110 and 121°C/230 and 250°F, keeping the temperature constant until the internal temperature is between 79 and 82°C/175 and 180°F. Remove the meat and cool to room temperature. Eat immediately or wrap and place in the refrigerator.

ALL-PURPOSE GAME MARINADE

Yield about 350 g/12 oz

3 Tbsp orange marmalade
50 ml/2 fl oz fresh lemon juice
50 ml/2 fl oz gin
50 ml/2 fl oz chicken or beef stock
50 ml/2 fl oz light soy sauce
1 Tbsp grated root ginger
1 Tbsp juniper berries, crushed
1 Tbsp grated lemon rind
3 cloves garlic, crushed
1 tsp dried basil
1 tsp black pepper
350 ml/12 fl oz olive oil

Combine the marmalade, lemon juice, gin, stock, ginger, juniper berries, lemon rind, garlic, basil and pepper in a blender or food processor fitted with a steel blade. Process for 30 seconds to break up the marmalade. With the motor running slowly, pour in the oil in a steady stream until it is all incorporated. Make the marinade on the day you are using it for the best results.

Smoked Pastrami

BAY SEASONING

Yield about 50 g/2 oz

2 Tbsp powdered bay leaf
2 Tbsp celery salt
1 Tbsp dry mustard
2 tsp finely ground black pepper
1 tsp white pepper
1 tsp ground nutmeg
1 tsp ground ginger
1 tsp paprika
1 tsp cayenne
¾ tsp ground cloves
½ tsp ground cardamom

Combine the bay leaf, celery salt, dry mustard, black pepper, white pepper, nutmeg, ginger, paprika, cayenne, cloves and cardamom. Blend well. Store in an airtight container in a cool dry place.

This seasoning can be used on almost any fish or seafood you want to smoke or grill. It is also good on chicken.

BROWN SUGAR/HONEY BACON CURE

Yield about 4.5 kg/10 lb home-made smoked bacon

450 g/1 lb sea or pickling salt (non-iodized)
450 g/1 lb dark brown sugar
50 g/2 oz mixed sodium nitrite (or dextrose) and non-iodized salt (available in health food stores or chemists), mixed 1:16
450 ml/16 fl oz honey
One 4.5- to 5-kg/10- to 11-lb piece fresh pork belly

Combine the salt and the brown sugar with the sodium nitrite and non-iodized salt mixture, and blend well. Rub the mixture all over the pork belly, (cut this into smaller pieces if wished) and place on a piece of clingfilm or greaseproof paper. Spread the honey all over the pork belly, then seal in the clingfilm. Place in the refrigerator and leave to cure for about a week.

Remove the pork belly from the refrigerator and unwrap. Wash the excess honey and salt mixture with warm water. Pat dry with kitchen paper. Leave to rest for 30 minutes at room temperature. Place the pork in a smoker preheated to between 82 and 93°C/180 and 200°F with the dampers wide open. Dry the bacon for about 10 to 15 minutes. Add wood to your heat source, close the dampers about one-third, and reduce the temperature to about 65°C/150°F, smoking at that temperature until the internal temperature is between 52 and 54°C/127 and 130°F.

Reduce the temperature of the smoker to between 49 and 52°C/120 and 125°F until the pork belly reaches the colour you want. Remove, cover and chill in the refrigerator overnight before slicing. Woods that work well for bacon are hickory and apple.

COACHES PORK PASTE

Yield about 450 g/1 lb

225 g/8 oz granulated sugar
225 g/8 oz dark brown sugar
50 g/2 oz seasoned salt
50 g/2 oz celery salt
50 g/2 oz paprika
25 g/1 oz chilli powder
2 Tbsp black pepper
1 Tbsp grated lemon rind
2 tsp toasted ground cumin
1 tsp onion powder
1 tsp garlic powder
50 to 100 ml/2 to 4 fl oz olive oil
2 to 4 Tbsp white wine vinegar

Combine the granulated sugar, brown sugar, seasoned salt, celery salt, paprika, chilli powder, black pepper, lemon rind, cumin, onion powder and garlic powder in a bowl and blend well. Blend in the olive oil; use enough to form a texture that looks like wet sand. Add white wine vinegar a little at a time until the paste reaches the thickness you want. Add more vinegar to form a thinner paste. Rub the mixture all over your pork joint or ribs. Place in a plastic bag and leave to marinate for 4 to 5 hours in the refrigerator. Cook as desired, hot- or smoke-roasted. This paste will keep covered in a refrigerator for months.

POMEGRANATE MARINADE FOR CHICKEN

Yield about 700 ml/1¼ pt

100 ml/4 fl oz pomegranate or
    cranberry juice
100 ml/4 fl oz orange juice
3 Tbsp fresh mint leaves
2 Tbsp Grand Marnier
1 Tbsp grated root ginger
2 cloves fresh garlic, crushed
1 tsp freshly ground black pepper
1 tsp sea salt
100 ml/4 fl oz walnut oil
225 ml/8 fl oz olive oil

Place the pomegranate juice, orange juice, mint, Grand Marnier, ginger, garlic, pepper and salt in a blender fitted with a steel blade. Combine the walnut and olive oil in a jug. Process on high and add the oil in a steady stream until it is all blended. This marinade is best used on the day it is made.

ALL-MEAT MARINADE

Yield about 450 ml/16 fl oz

300 ml/10 fl oz cider vinegar
175 ml/6 fl oz sunflower oil
2 Tbsp mustard powder
1 Tbsp chilli powder
1 Tbsp light brown sugar
1 Tbsp sea salt
1 tsp toasted ground cumin
1 tsp paprika
1 tsp finely ground black pepper
4 large cloves garlic, crushed
1 to 2 Tbsp hot sauce

Combine the vinegar, oil, mustard, chilli powder, sugar, salt, cumin, paprika, pepper, garlic and hot sauce in a bowl, blending with a wire whisk. Best used on the day made.

SALMON BRINE

Yield about 3.6 l/6½ pt

450 g/1 lb brown sugar
125 g/4 oz sea or pickling salt
225 ml/8 fl oz soy sauce
225 ml/8 fl oz dry white wine
1 tsp onion flakes
1 tsp garlic powder
1 tsp white pepper
1 Tbsp Tabasco sauce or to taste
3 l/5¼ pt water

Combine the brown sugar, salt, soy sauce, white wine, onions, garlic, white pepper, Tabasco sauce and water in a bowl and blend well.

Cover the salmon with the brine, making sure that it is submerged; brine for 2 hours in the refrigerator or overnight. The unused brine will keep in the refrigerator for months. Remove the salmon from the brine and rinse with cold water. Season with whatever seasoning you like and smoke until the fish flakes easily.

Pomegranate Marinade

JERK SEASONING

Yield about 40 g/1½ oz

2 Tbsp salt (non-iodized)
1 Tbsp granulated sugar
2 tsp ground chilli or 1 tsp ground
   chilli and 1 tsp cayenne
2 tsp onion powder
2 tsp garlic powder
1½ tsp ground allspice
1 tsp ground ginger
1 tsp finely ground black pepper
½ tsp ground cinnamon
¼ tsp ground cloves
¼ tsp ground nutmeg

Combine the salt, sugar, chilli, onion, garlic, allspice, ginger, pepper, cinnamon, cloves and nutmeg in a small bowl and blend well. Store in an airtight container in a cool dry place.

If you like the flavour of the Scotch Bonnet peppers but not all of the heat use 1 teaspoon Scotch Bonnet pepper and 1 teaspoon cayenne. It still has a good bite, but won't be as pungent. If you like more fire use 2 tablespoons of Scotch Bonnet pepper.

HONEY BRINE FOR TURKEY OR CHICKEN

Yield just over 3.6 l/6½ pt

125 g/4 oz pickling or
   non-iodized salt
225 g/8 oz dark brown sugar
100 ml/4 fl oz clear honey
1 Tbsp meat tenderizer
1 Tbsp white pepper
2 tsp ground ginger
2 tsp powdered bay leaf
1 tsp ground allspice
1 tsp ground clove
1 tsp mace
1 gallon water

Combine the salt, sugar, honey, meat tenderizer, pepper, ginger, bay leaf, allspice, clove, mace and water in a saucepan. Bring to the boil, stirring to dissolve the sugar and honey. Reduce the heat and simmer for about 15 minutes. Set aside and allow to cool.

Rinse your turkey or chicken with cold water. Place in a non-reactive container, pour the brine over the bird and place a weight on the bird to hold it under the brine. Refrigerate for 4 to 8 hours or overnight. Rinse the bird with cold water and pat dry with kitchen paper. Season inside and out with your favourite rub or seasoning. Cook, smoke then smoke-roast, barbecue, or deep-fry.

CHINESE BARBECUE SEASONING OR RUB

Yield about 125 g/4 oz

3 Tbsp granulated sugar
2 Tbsp paprika
1 Tbsp dark brown sugar
1 Tbsp garlic salt
1 Tbsp seasoned salt
1 Tbsp celery salt
1 Tbsp onion salt
2 Tbsp chilli powder
1 Tbsp finely Szechuan ground
   pepper
1 Tbsp finely ground black pepper
1 Tbsp dry mustard
2 tsp ground ginger
1 tsp Chinese five-spice powder
1 tsp cayenne

Combine the sugar, paprika, brown sugar, garlic salt, seasoned salt, celery salt, onion salt, chilli powder, Szechuan pepper, black pepper, mustard, ginger, five-spice powder and cayenne in a sieve and sift into a bowl. Blend well. Store in an airtight container in a cool dry place.

Mexican Chipotle Marinade

Yield about 400 ml/4 fl oz

8 tinned chipotle peppers in
  adobo or tomato sauce
2 Tbsp tomato purée
225 ml/8 fl oz fresh orange juice
3 Tbsp fresh lime juice
2 Tbsp red wine vinegar
1 Tbsp ketchup
4 large cloves garlic, diced
8-cm/3-in piece orange rind
1 tsp dried oregano
1 tsp toasted ground cumin
1 tsp sea salt
1 tsp black pepper

Place the chipotles, tomato purée, orange juice, lime juice, vinegar, ketchup, garlic, orange rind, oregano, cumin, salt and pepper in a saucepan. Bring to the boil. Reduce the heat to a vigorous simmer until the sauce is reduced by one-third. Transfer to a blender fitted with a stainless steel blade, and purée until smooth. Leave to cool. This is a good marinade for pork and chicken. For the best flavour, use immediately.

Red Wine Marinade for Game

Yield about 700 ml/1¼ pt

450 ml/16 fl oz red wine
3 Tbsp red wine vinegar
1 small onion, finely chopped
1 small carrot, grated
4 to 6 cloves garlic, crushed
2 bay leaves
2 tsp rubbed sage
1 tsp juniper berries, mashed
1 tsp whole cloves

Combine all the ingredients in a saucepan and bring to the boil. Reduce the heat and simmer for 30 minutes. Leave to cool before using. Marinate venison steaks for 3 to 4 hours and roasting joints for 6 to 8 hours or overnight in the refrigerator.

Hot-smoking and Stove-top Smoking Recipes

I FIRST BECAME interested in hot-smoking at a very young age, watching my father, along with my grandfather and uncles practise the art. Cooking with wood and charcoal really is like learning an art or craft. There is also something special about cooking for your family, friends or work colleagues. As people enjoy the flavour of your smoked product (and you enjoy the praise!), you will achieve a real sense of accomplishment.

For anyone interested in getting into smoking, stove-top smoking is a great way to start. First, the equipment can cost next to nothing; you need a pan, a rack, wood chips or sawdust, and a tight-fitting lid or cover, which can simply be a piece of metal or foil. Now for the sheer pleasure of it and a great learning experience, pick out one of the recipes and see how easy it is to start smoking.

CHICKEN WITH CHAMPAGNE SAUCE

Serves 8

Eight 150-g/5-oz boneless, skinless
    chicken breasts
3 Tbsp fresh lemon juice
1 Tbsp coarse salt
1 Tbsp finely ground black pepper
4 fresh peaches, peeled, stoned
    and thinly sliced

FOR THE SAUCE

125 g/4 oz unsalted butter
1 red onion, grated
3 Tbsp plain flour
200 g/7 oz peaches, puréed
⅕ bottle Champagne
2 Tbsp peach brandy

Sprinkle the chicken breasts with the lemon juice. Season with the salt and pepper and top with the peach slices. Place the chicken and peach on your cooker and smoke, using your favourite fruitwood, for 1 to 1½ hours.

In a saucepan over medium-hot heat add the butter and sauté the onions until soft but not browned. Blend in the flour and cook, stirring for 2 to 3 minutes. Do not let it brown. Stir in the peaches, Champagne and peach brandy and heat until the sauce has thickened. Spoon over the grilled chicken breasts and serve with spinach noodles.

SHANGHAI SMOKED CHICKEN

Serves 2 to 4

FOR THE MARINADE

100 ml/4 fl oz soy sauce
2 Tbsp sunflower oil
2 Tbsp hoisin sauce
2 heaped Tbsp brown sugar
2 Tbsp sherry
1 Tbsp grated root ginger
1 tsp sea salt
2 spring onions, finely chopped

One 1.4 to 1.8-kg/3 to 4-lb whole
    chicken, butterflied

Combine the soy sauce, oil, hoisin sauce, sugar, sherry, ginger, salt and spring onions in a bowl and blend with a wire whisk.

Butterflying the chicken can be done with a paring knife. Place the chicken on its breast; cut down both sides of the backbone and remove. The only bones you have to cut are tiny rib bones. Open the chicken up, cut the piece of white gristle, and, placing your thumbs on either side of the breastbone, pull out the breastbone and the piece of white gristle at the base and back of the breast. Place the chicken in a large zip-lock type plastic bag. Pour the marinade over the chicken and marinate for 2 to 4 hours in the refrigerator.

Remove the chicken from the marinade, place on your cooker and smoke for 3 to 4 hours or until the internal temperature in the breast or thigh reads 71°C/160°F, or the juices run clear.

Chicken with Champagne Sauce

SMOKED CHICKEN AND RICE SALAD

Serves 4

Four 150-g/5-oz boneless, skinless
   chicken breasts
Non-stick cooking spray
1 Tbsp black pepper
1 Tbsp grated lemon rind
1 Tbsp garlic salt
125 g/4 oz wild rice
150 g/5 oz brown rice
175 ml/6 fl oz water

FOR THE SALAD DRESSING

150 ml/6 fl oz bottled Italian
   salad dressing
100 ml/4 fl oz mayonnaise
1 Tbsp hot sauce
2 tsp Worcestershire sauce
1 tsp sea salt
1 tsp freshly ground black pepper
50 g/2 oz pecans, roasted and
   chopped
6 spring onions, chopped
¹/₂ tsp paprika

Spray the chicken breast all over with the cooking spray. Combine the black pepper, lemon rind and garlic salt in a bowl and blend well. Season the chicken with the mixture. Place in a stove-top smoker with wood chips of your choice and smoke until cooked, 30 to 40 minutes. Remove from the smoker and set aside on a plate.

Place the water in a saucepan with a tight-fitting lid. Combine the rice and water and bring to the boil, stirring. Reduce the heat, cover and simmer until the rice is cooked.

In a medium bowl combine the Italian dressing, mayonnaise, hot sauce, Worcestershire sauce, salt and pepper and blend with a wire whisk. Cover and set aside.

This salad can be served hot or chilled. Dice or cut the chicken breasts into chunks or strips, mix with the wild rice mixture and toss. Add the nuts and spring onions, top with dressing, sprinkle with paprika, mix gently and serve.

TEA-SMOKED DUCK WITH FRAGRANT RICE

Serves 2 to 4

3 Tbsp coarse salt
1 Tbsp peppercorns
One 2.3-kg/5-lb duckling, dressed
   and rinsed
6 spring onions, trimmed
1 Tbsp grated root ginger
175 g/6 oz white rice
3 Tbsp black tea leaves
50 g/2 oz granulated sugar

Add the salt and peppercorns to a dry heavy frying pan and heat over moderate heat until the peppercorns are fragrant. Leave to cool then place in a teatowel and crush with a rolling pin or a wood mallet.

Flatten the duck slightly by pressing down on the breastbone to break it. Rub the duck inside and out with the salt and peppercorn mixture. Place the duck in a large roasting tin, invert a plate on top, and weight the duck down with a heavy brick or weight covered with clingfilm. Marinate for 1 to 2 days.

Rinse the duck. Put the spring onions and ginger in the cavity. Steam or boil the duck until tender, 1 to 1½ hours. (Boiling is faster, but steaming produces a better result.) Remove the duck and drain.

Line a roasting tin or wok with foil. Combine the rice, tea leaves and sugar in a small bowl and pour over the foil. Place the duck on a rack over the tea mixture and seal the tin as tightly as possible. If you cover the pan with clingfilm and then foil you get a better seal.

Set the tin over high heat for 5 minutes. Reduce the heat to medium and heat for 15 to 20 minutes. Remove from the heat and leave to rest, uncovered, for 30 minutes. Leave to cool. Chop the duck into 2.5- to 5-centimetre/1- to 2-inch pieces, bones and all, and cut the meat into strips. Serve at room temperature with the fragrant rice and your favourite barbecue or dipping sauce to the side.

Fragrant rice

Serves 6 to 8

225 g/8 oz white rice
5 Tbsp groundnut oil
2 Tbsp grated root ginger
1 Tbsp crushed garlic
3 Tbsp diced red pepper
6 spring onions, chopped
3 Tbsp soy sauce
1 Tbsp granulated sugar
1 tsp sea salt
450 ml/16 fl oz water

Heat the oil in a saucepan that has a tight-fitting lid. Add the rice and brown, stirring constantly, taking care not to burn. Add the ginger and garlic and sauté for a further minute. Add the red pepper and onion, sauté for a further 30 seconds, stir in the soy sauce, sugar and salt and cook for a further minute. Add the water and bring to the boil. Reduce the heat and cook until the rice is soft and tender.

Smoked Chicken Breast Sandwich
with Basil Olive Pesto

Serves 8

FOR THE MARINADE

50 ml/2 fl oz fresh lemon juice
50 ml/2 fl oz balsamic vinegar
4 cloves garlic, crushed
1 tsp dried oregano
1 tsp black pepper
1 tsp grated lemon rind
1 tsp salt
50 ml/2 fl oz virgin olive oil

**Eight 150-g/5-oz boneless, skinless
 chicken breasts**
450 ml/16 fl oz boiling water
**80 to 125 g/3 to 4 oz sun-dried
 tomatoes, not packed in oil**
One 50-cm/20-in loaf Italian bread
100 ml/4 fl oz basil olive pesto
**1 small packet rocket leaves,
 washed and dried**

Combine the lemon juice, vinegar, garlic, oregano, black pepper, grated lemon rind and salt in a bowl and beat in the oil with a wire whisk until well blended. Place the chicken breasts in a zip-lock type plastic bag or a non-reactive baking tin. Pour the marinade over the chicken, cover and marinate for 2 to 4 hours in the refrigerator.

Remove the chicken breasts from the marinade and place on the rack in the pan smoker. Add wood chips and heat until the chips start to smoke. Cover with the lid and smoke for about 30 minutes or until cooked.

In a heatproof bowl pour the boiling water over the tomatoes, cover and leave to stand for 20 to 30 minutes or until soft. Drain the tomatoes and pat dry.

Cut the loaf of bread in half horizontally and spread with basil olive pesto. Slice the chicken breasts and place on the bottom half of the loaf, top with tomatoes and arugula, cover with the top of the loaf and secure with cocktail sticks.

Basil olive pesto

Yield about 175 ml/6 fl oz

2 cloves garlic, chopped
**1 large handful (about 40 g/1¹⁄₂ oz)
 fresh basil leaves, rinsed and
 patted dry**
**1 large handful (about 40 g/1¹⁄₂ oz)
 fresh flat-leaf parsley, finely
 chopped**
50 g/2 oz pine nuts
50 ml/2 fl oz olive oil
**40 g/1¹⁄₄ oz Kalamata or other
 brine-cured olives, stoned and
 finely chopped**

Place the garlic in a running food processor. Add the basil, parsley and nuts and blend well. Add the oil in a thin stream and blend until smooth. Transfer to a bowl and stir in the olives. Use at room temperature.

Lamb Sausages with Basque Haricot Bean Stew and Mixed Green Salad

Makes 2.3 kg/5 lb

1.4 kg/3 lb minced lamb
900 g/2 lb minced pork or beef
2 Tbsp dried mint
1 Tbsp garlic powder
1 Tbsp seasoned salt
1 Tbsp hot red pepper flakes
2 tsp finely ground black pepper
2 tsp onion powder
1 tsp dried savory
$\frac{1}{2}$ tsp mace

Combine the mint, garlic, salt, crushed red peppers, black pepper, onion, savory and mace in a small bowl and blend well.

Mix the minced lamb and pork together in a large bowl. Add the seasoning a third at a time and blend in thoroughly.

Form into sausage shapes. Place on smoker and smoke for 2 to 3 hours or until the internal temperature is 71°C/160°F, turning the sausages about halfway through the cooking process.

Basque haricot bean stew

Serves 8 to 10

275 g/10 oz dried haricot beans
1 large leek, cut in half lengthways
 and rinsed
1 green pepper, seeded and halved
1 sweet red pepper, seeded and
 halved
3 Tbsp olive oil
2 onions, diced
1 Tbsp paprika
1 tsp sea salt
1 tsp freshly ground black pepper

Rinse the beans in cold water. Place the beans in a large bowl and cover with 2.5 to 5 centremetres/1 to 2 inches of cold water. Soak for at least 8 hours or overnight. Drain the beans and rinse again. Place in a large stockpot.

Add the leek and peppers to the pot and pour in enough cold water to cover the beans and vegetables by 5 to 8 centimetres/2 to 3 inches. Bring to the boil and cook rapidly for 2 to 3 minutes, skimming the foam from the surface. Reduce the heat and simmer for about 2 hours. Add about 50 to 100 ml/2 to 4 fl oz cold water every half hour. Simmer until the beans are tender.

In a heavy-bottomed frying pan, heat the oil over a medium heat. Add the onions and sauté until they are soft, about 8 to 10 minutes. Add the paprika and cook for a further 2 minutes. Add to the beans and season with the salt and pepper.

Discard the leek and peppers if preferred, or chop up and return to the beans stirring to mix.

Mixed green salad with green goddess dressing

Serves 8 to 10

1 small head Cos lettuce, chopped
 or torn
2 heads butterhead lettuce,
 chopped or torn
3 Tbsp mayonnaise
3 Tbsp chopped chives
2 Tbsp plain yoghurt
2 Tbsp Dijon mustard
1 Tbsp white wine vinegar
1 Tbsp fresh tarragon leaves,
 chopped
1 Tbsp fresh parsley, chopped
1 tsp anchovy paste or to taste
1 tsp sea salt
$1/2$ tsp white pepper
1 bunch watercress, stems removed
 and rinsed
1 red onion, diced
1 cucumber, peeled, seeded and
 diced
175 g/6 oz cherry tomatoes, rinsed
 and halved

Rinse the lettuces and pat dry with a teatowel. Combine the mayonnaise, chives, yoghurt, mustard, vinegar, tarragon, parsley, anchovy paste, salt and pepper in a bowl and blend well with a wire whisk.

In a large bowl combine the watercress, Cos, butterhead, onion, cucumber and cherry tomatoes, and blend well. Serve the salad and either spoon the dressing over or serve on the side.

WOOD-ROASTED SWEET RED PEPPERS

Serves 4 to 6

3 medium sweet red peppers
One 2.5-cm/1-in piece grapevine
  cutting
5 cloves garlic, thinly sliced
3 Tbsp extra-virgin olive oil
1 Tbsp boiling water
2 tsp paprika
1 tsp granulated sugar
1/2 tsp sea salt

Roast the peppers directly over a gas flame, under a grill or over hot charcoal, turning frequently until charred all over. Place the peppers in a paper bag and seal. Set aside for 10 minutes to steam. Scrape off the blackened skin and remove the cores, seeds and ribs. Rinse the peppers and pat dry with kitchen paper.

Place the grapevine cutting in the bottom of your stove-top smoker; place the rack over the cutting. Heat until the grapevine starts smoking, about 3 minutes. Place the peppers on the rack, cover and smoke for 5 minutes. Remove the peppers, place on a plate or tray and leave to cool slightly. Slice into 1-cm/1/2-in wide slices.

In a heavy frying pan, cook the garlic in the olive oil over medium heat until slightly soft, about 2 minutes. Add the pepper strips, reduce the heat to low and cook for 10 to 15 minutes, stirring occasionally. In a small bowl combine the paprika, sugar, salt and water and set aside. When the peppers are ready, add the paprika water and cook for a further 5 to 10 minutes. Serve warm or at room temperature, drizzled with a little olive oil, or use to top focaccia bread.

RATATOUILLE PARCELS

Serves 6 to 8

1 medium aubergine, peeled and
   cubed
1 large red onion, peeled and cut
   into 4-cm/1½-in pieces
1 large red pepper, seeded and cut
   into 4-cm/1½-in pieces
1 large yellow pepper, seeded and
   cut into 4-cm/1½-in pieces
1 medium courgette, quartered and
   cut into 2.5-cm/1-in pieces
4 large cloves garlic, crushed
3 Tbsp olive oil
4 medium tomatoes, peeled, seeded
   and cut into bite-sized pieces
3 Tbsp fresh basil leaves, chopped
3 Tbsp fresh lemon juice
2 Tbsp capers
2 Tbsp chopped fresh flat-leaf
   parsley
2 Tbsp chopped fresh curly parsley
1 tsp sea salt
1 tsp freshly ground black pepper

Combine the aubergine, onion, red pepper, yellow pepper, courgette and garlic in a large bowl. Pour the olive oil over the vegetables and toss to coat. Place in a 23 x 32.5-cm/9 x 13-in baking dish and cover with clingfilm, then with foil to seal. Place on your cooker and cook for about 1 hour. Combine the tomatoes, basil, lemon juice, capers, both types of parsley, salt and pepper and toss to mix. Remove the dish from the cooker and take off the foil and clingfilm. Add the tomato mixture and blend together. Place back in your cooker and add wood chips or other smoking material to your fire and smoke, stirring occasionally, for a further hour or until done to your liking.

TERIYAKI ONIONS

Serves 6 to 8

FOR THE TERIYAKI SAUCE

450 ml/16 fl oz pineapple juice
350 ml/12 fl oz soy sauce
225 g/8 oz granulated sugar
1 Tbsp grated root ginger
2 cloves garlic, crushed
1 Tbsp arrowroot or
   2¼ tsp cornflour
2 Tbsp cold water

6 to 8 small or medium onions

First make the sauce. Place the pineapple juice, soy sauce, sugar, ginger and garlic in a saucepan and bring to the boil over a medium heat, stirring to dissolve and incorporate the sugar. Take care not to let the mixture boil over. Combine the arrowroot and cold water in a small bowl and make a paste. Add to the boiling mixture, stirring with a wire whisk. Bring back to the boil. Reduce the heat and simmer until a sheen forms, about 2 minutes. Remove from the heat and set aside.

Peel the onions and using a sharp, thin knife cut down to the root core, but not through it. Repeat this cut at least 7 more times. Place each onion in the centre of a foil sheet and bring the sides of the foil up around the onion. Pour 3 tablespoons teriyaki sauce over each onion and twist the foil to seal. Place the foil parcels on your cooker and cook for at least 1½ hours, longer if desired. The timing is not critical because if the onions are sweet you can eat them raw, cold or hot. Remove the onions from their foil parcels and they will look like open flowers. Serve the remainder of the sauce on the side or top with a tablespoon of sauce.

POTATO, PEA AND MUSHROOM PARCELS

Serves 8

4 large russet potatoes, washed and
   dried
125 g/4 oz butter, sliced into 8 even
   pieces, more if preferred
225 g/8 oz frozen peas, defrosted
175 g/6 oz fresh mushrooms, sliced
2 tsp sea salt
1 tsp freshly ground black pepper

Cut the potatoes in half lengthways. Slice each half into about 3-millimetre/1/8-inch slices and place in the centre of a 30 x 30-centimetre/12 x 12-inch piece of foil. Top the potatoes with a knob of butter, 25 g/1 oz peas, and mushroom slices. Season the potatoes to taste with salt and pepper. Seal the foil parcels, place on your cooker and cook for 1 to 2 hours or until the potatoes are cooked.

SMOKED AUBERGINE PARCEL

Serves 6 to 8

3 Tbsp extra-virgin olive oil
2 Tbsp fresh lemon juice
4 large cloves garlic, crushed
1 tsp sea salt
1/2 tsp freshly ground black pepper
1 large aubergine, about 700 g/
   1 1/2 lb, cut into 1-cm/1/2-in slices
1/2 tsp dried thyme

Combine the olive oil, lemon juice, garlic, salt and pepper in a small bowl and blend well. Dip the sliced aubergine into the mixture and place in the centre of a large piece of foil. Pour the remaining marinade over the slices and season with the thyme. Seal the foil parcel, folding over several times to ensure it is airtight. Place on your cooker and cook for about 1 hour. Carefully open the foil parcel and roll down the sides to form a dish. If there is too much liquid in the parcel, drain some of it off. Add smoking wood chips to the coals and smoke for a further 1/2 to 1 hour to obtain a smoke flavour.

WHISKY-MUSTARD GLAZED HAM

Serves 12 to 15

One 6.8-kg/15-lb pre-cooked
   smoked ham on the bone
Whole cloves

FOR THE GLAZE

225 g/8 oz Dijon mustard
450 g/1 lb dark brown sugar
5 Tbsp whisky
1 tsp sea salt
1 tsp fresh ground black pepper

Trim the skin and excess fat from the ham. With a sharp knife score the ham fat in 2.5-centimetre/1-inch squares. Place a whole clove in the centre of each square. If you have trouble inserting the clove into the ham, pierce the hole with a skewer or cocktail stick.

Place the ham in your cooker and smoke for 5 to 8 hours, longer if wished. After the ham has been in the cooker at least 4 hours, combine the mustard, brown sugar, whisky, salt and pepper in a bowl with a heavy spoon or wire whisk. Brush this glaze over the ham with a pastry brush or, if preferred, spoon it on.

PAN-SMOKED SALMON WITH ASPARAGUS AND MUSHROOMS

Serves 4 to 6

225 ml/8 fl oz mayonnaise

2 Tbsp balsamic vinegar

One 1.4-kg/3-lb salmon fillet, with pin bones removed

1 Tbsp bay seasoning (see page 26)

2 Tbsp fresh dill

3 Tbsp sesame oil

2 tsp grated root ginger

2 large cloves garlic, crushed

2 shallots, thinly sliced

225 g/8 oz chestnut or small oyster mushrooms, stems removed

2 Tbsp fish sauce

1 Tbsp soy sauce

1 tsp granulated sugar

700 to 900 g/1½ to 2 lb fresh asparagus

2 tsp olive oil

In a small bowl combine the mayonnaise and balsamic vinegar, blending well. Season the salmon with the bay seasoning, top with the mayonnaise mixture and top that with the dill. Place hickory wood chips or any other wood chips of your choice in the smoker. Place the rack in the bottom and heat until the chips start to smoke, then place the fish on the rack, cover and smoke 20 to 40 minutes or until the fish flakes easily.

Heat the sesame oil in a frying pan over a medium heat and sauté the ginger, garlic and shallots for about 2 minutes, stirring constantly. Add the mushrooms, fish sauce, soy sauce and sugar and cook, stirring occasionally, until the mushrooms are soft. Set aside and keep warm.

Trim the asparagus and cut the tough stalks. Lightly brush or spray a grill pan with oil then place on moderate heat until hot. Add the asparagus and cook, turning occasionally for 10 minutes or until they begin to char.

To serve, carefully divide the salmon into 4 to 6 portions. Divide the asparagus and top with the mushroom mixture. Serve warm.

SCALLOP AND PRAWN BROCHETTES
WITH CURRIED RICE PILAF

Serves 6 to 8

450 to 900 g/1 to 2 lb scallops,
  shucked and rinsed
450 to 900 g/1 to 2 lb prawns,
  peeled and deveined
225 g/8 oz butter, melted
2 Tbsp fresh lemon juice
2 tsp freshly ground black pepper
1 tsp paprika
1 lemon, cut into wedges

FOR THE MARINADE

225 ml/8 fl oz dry white wine
2 Tbsp balsamic vinegar
2 Tbsp fresh lemon juice
3 Tbsp sunflower oil
1 Tbsp chopped fresh tarragon
1 tsp chopped fresh basil
1 tsp chopped fresh thyme
1 tsp chopped fresh oregano
1 tsp granulated sugar
1 tsp sea salt
1 tsp freshly ground black pepper

For the marinade combine the wine, vinegar, lemon juice, oil, tarragon, basil, thyme, oregano, sugar, salt and pepper in a non-reactive bowl and blend well with a wire whisk. Place the scallops and prawns in the marinade, tossing to coat evenly. Cover and marinate for 2 to 4 hours in the refrigerator.

Drain the marinated scallops and prawns and thread them onto long metal skewers, threading the scallops through their diameter. Combine the melted butter and lemon juice. Brush the scallops and prawns with the butter mixture and season with pepper and paprika. Place on your cooker and smoke for 30 minutes to 1 hour or until cooked, basting with the butter-lemon mixture every 15 minutes. Serve with lemon wedges.

Curried rice pilaf

Serves 6 to 8

2 Tbsp olive oil
25 g/1 oz butter
3 cloves garlic, crushed
300 g/10 oz converted
  (par-boiled) rice
2 chicken stock cubes
1 small red onion, diced

1 stalk celery, diced
$\frac{1}{2}$ pimento, diced
1 Tbsp curry powder
1 tsp black pepper
700 mk/1$\frac{1}{4}$ pt water
6 spring onions, thinly sliced

Heat the olive oil and butter over a medium heat and sauté the garlic, stirring constantly. Add the rice and crumble in the chicken stock cubes. Sauté until golden brown, stirring frequently so the rice does not scorch. Add the onions, celery, pimento, curry powder and pepper and cook, stirring, for 2 minutes. Pour in the water and bring to the boil. Add the spring onions, cover and simmer for 5 minutes. Remove from the heat and leave to stand for 30 minutes. Serve warm.

SPICED POUSSINS
WITH CITRUS ORZO

Serves 8 to 10

2 Tbsp roasted cumin seeds
One 8-cm/3-in cinnamon stick,
    broken into pieces
8 whole cloves
3 Tbsp paprika
2 tsp granulated sugar
1 tsp cayenne
1 tsp sea salt
4 large cloves garlic, crushed
1 tsp sea salt
1 Tbsp grated lemon rind
Juice of 1 lemon
3 Tbsp olive oil
Eight 350-g/12-oz poussins or
    2 whole 1.4-kg/3-lb chickens
50 g/2 oz unsalted butter
2 Tbsp fresh parsley, chopped

FOR THE SAUCE

450 ml/16 fl oz Melba sauce
    (raspberry sauce)
25 g/1 oz butter
1 to 2 Tbsp Grand Marnier
2 Tbsp cold water (optional)
1 Tbsp cornflour (optional)

Put the cumin seeds, cinnamon and cloves in a spice grinder or pestle and mortar and grind. Combine the ground spices with the paprika, sugar, cayenne and salt, blending well. Work the garlic and salt to a paste. Combine the garlic paste, lemon rind, lemon juice, oil and two tablespoons of the spice mixture (reserve the remainder) in a non-reactive bowl and blend well.

If you are using whole chickens, cut into quarters. Rub the poussins or chicken pieces all over with the garlic marinade. Place in a glass baking dish, cover and leave to marinate for at least 2 hours, but no longer than 4 hours, in the refrigerator.

To cook, place on your smoker, skin-side up or breast-up if using poussins and season with the reserved spice mixture. Melt the butter in a small saucepan and combine with the parsley. Cook for two hours, basting with the butter mixture every 20 minutes for the last hour. Poussins are cooked when they reach an internal temperature of 71°C/160°F or when the juices run clear.

To make the sauce, combine the Melba sauce, butter and Grand Marnier in a saucepan and bring to a fast simmer. Do not boil. If you want a thicker sauce combine the cornflour and cold water and blend in with a wire whisk until thick and glossy.

Citrus orzo

450 g/1 lb orzo (or risotto rice)
1.6 l/2³⁄₄ pt chicken stock
1 Tbsp olive oil
3 Tbsp fresh lemon juice
3 Tbsp chopped fresh basil
3 Tbsp chopped fresh parsley
3 Tbsp chopped fresh mint
1 Tbsp grated lemon rind
1 tsp sea salt
1 tsp freshly ground black pepper

Bring the chicken stock to the boil in a large saucepan. Add the orzo and cook, stirring often to prevent sticking, until most of the stock is absorbed and the orzo is tender and creamy, about 10 minutes. Remove from the heat and stir in the oil, lemon juice, basil, parsley, mint and lemon rind. Season with the salt and pepper. Serve warm.

Serve the poussins with citrus orzo and sauce on the side.

Halibut with Breadcrumbs and Smoke-roasted Tomato Sauce

Serves 4

80 g/3 oz fresh white breadcrumbs
2 Tbsp chopped fresh tarragon

FOR THE SAUCE

75 ml/3 fl oz extra-virgin olive oil
450 g/1 lb plum tomatoes, halved and
    seeded
1 head garlic
3 Tbsp balsamic vinegar
2 tsp granulated sugar
1 tsp sea salt
1 tsp freshly ground black pepper
3 Tbsp mayonnaise
2 tsp Dijon mustard
Four 175-g/6-oz fresh halibut fillets
2 Tbsp sea salt
1 Tbsp freshly ground black pepper
1 Tbsp fresh tarragon leaves

In a small bowl combine the breadcrumbs and tarragon and blend well. Cover and set aside.

Place the olive oil in a large bowl. Add the tomatoes and garlic, tossing to coat evenly. Place the tomatoes and garlic on the rack of a smoking dish. Add 3 tablespoons hickory sawdust or chips and heat over a high heat until the chips start to smoke, about 3 minutes. Cover, reduce the heat and smoke for about 20 to 30 minutes or until the tomatoes are lightly browned and the garlic is tender when pierced with a knife. (The garlic may take a little longer, 10 to 15 minutes.) Peel the garlic and place in a blender fitted with a steel blade, add the tomatoes, vinegar, sugar, salt and pepper and purée until smooth. Add some water if the sauce seems too thick. Place in a saucepan and warm. Set aside and keep warm.

Combine the mayonnaise and mustard in a small bowl. Season the fillets all over with salt and pepper. Spread the mayonnaise mixture over the top of the fillets and pat the seasoned breadcrumbs evenly on top. Place in your smoking dish and smoke with wood chips of your choice for 10 to 15 minutes or until the fish flakes easily. Serve with fresh tarragon sprinkled over.

SMOKE-ROASTING RECIPES

SMOKE-ROASTING is by far is my favourite method. There are several rules that will make your smoke-roasting a success. The first one is to have fun and enjoy yourself! The second is to keep records of quantities and cooking times for future reference, and finally, it is important to maintain as constant a temperature as possible during cooking.

For those unfamiliar with smoking, these recipes have been written to ensure that you succeed the very first time you try them. You will gain great satisfaction from knowing that this great food has been produced by your very own hands, which have learnt to apply spices and seasonings, and to control the temperature and level of smoke.

Pork Tenderloin Havana

with Black Bean Sauce and Fried Plantains

Serves 8 to 10

FOR THE MARINADE

3 oranges
4 limes
225 ml/8 fl oz olive oil
1 Tbsp grated orange rind
1 Tbsp grated lime rind
2 tsp hot red pepper flakes
1 tsp coarse salt
6 Tbsp chopped fresh coriander
2 bay leaves, crushed
3 Tbsp sherry vinegar
Lime or sour orange wedges, soured
  cream and sliced red onions

Four 450-g/1-lb pork tenderloins,
  trimmed of membrane and fat

Roll the oranges and limes on your worktop, this will release more juice from them. Cut and squeeze the oranges and limes into a large non-reactive bowl, then peel and chop the fruit. Add the fruit, olive oil, rind, crushed red peppers, salt, coriander and bay leaves and mix well. Place the pork in a glass baking dish or self-locking plastic bag and pour the marinade over, making sure that the meat is evenly coated. Cover or seal and marinate for 8 hours or overnight in the refrigerator.

Remove the meat from the marinade and place on your cooker. Smoke for 2 to 3 hours or until it reaches a temperature of 62 to 71°C/145 to 160°F. To serve, slice into 1-cm/¹/₂-inch slices, top with bean sauce and sprinkle over the sherry vinegar. Serve with the fried plantains and garnish with lime or sour orange wedges, soured cream and red onion slices.

Black bean sauce

Serves 8 to 10

125 g/4 oz bacon, diced
3 Tbsp groundnut oil
1 red onion, diced
1 medium jalapeño chilli, diced
2 stalks celery, diced
300 g/10 oz black beans, soaked in water overnight
3 Tbsp roasted ground cumin
1 tsp cayenne
1 bay leaf
1 tsp black pepper
1.8 l/3¼ pt chicken stock
1 to 2 Tbsp sea salt

In a large saucepan sauté the bacon squares in the oil until almost cooked. Add the onions, jalapeño and celery and cook until soft. Drain the beans and cook for 2 minutes, stirring. Add the cumin, cayenne, bay leaf and pepper and stir. Add the stock and bring to the boil. Cook the beans until soft. Adjust the seasoning if necessary. Set aside and keep warm.

Fried plantains

Serves 8 to 10

1 to 2 plantains, peeled and cut on an extreme
    bias into 1-cm/½-in slices
125 g/4 oz plain flour
1 tsp ground cinnamon
1 tsp freshly ground black pepper
1 tsp sea salt
3 Tbsp clarified butter

Dredge the plantains in the flour, seasoned with cinnamon, pepper and salt. Gently sauté the plantains in the clarified butter until golden brown. Drain on kitchen paper until ready to serve. If necessary sauté the plantains again to crisp them up before serving.

Chinese Barbecued Pork

Serves 6 to 8

FOR THE MARINADE

225 ml/8 fl oz soy sauce

3 Tbsp hoisin sauce

3 heaped Tbsp light brown sugar

2 Tbsp clear honey

2 Tbsp sherry

2 tsp grated root ginger

1 large clove garlic, crushed

1 Tbsp red food colouring (optional)

1 tsp ground cinnamon

$\frac{1}{2}$ tsp Chinese five-spice powder

Spring onion curls to garnish

**Four 450-g/1-lb pork tenderloins,
   trimmed of membrane and fat**

Combine the soy sauce, hoisin sauce, sugar, honey, sherry, ginger, garlic, food colouring, cinnamon and five-spice powder in a bowl and blend well. Place the tenderloins in a non-reactive dish or plastic bag and pour the marinade over them. Marinate for 2 to 4 hours in the refrigerator, turning occasionally. Remove the tenderloins from the marinade, reserving the marinade, and place on your cooker. Smoke until the internal temperature reaches 62 to 71°C/145 to 165°F. Do not overcook. Baste with the reserved marinade every 30 minutes. Serve hot or cold, cut on a diagonal on a bed of spring onion curls, as a main course, starter, Chinese salad or sandwich filling.

Use hoisin and chilli sauce for dipping, if you like.

GUAVA-GLAZED BABY BACK RIBS

Serves 8 to 10

FOR THE DRY RUB

50 g/2 oz brown sugar
50 g/2 oz granulated sugar
2 Tbsp seasoned salt
2 Tbsp garlic salt
2 Tbsp celery salt
2 Tbsp chilli powder
2 Tbsp finely ground black pepper
1 tsp ground allspice
1 tsp ground ginger
1/2 tsp cayenne
1/4 tsp ground cloves
1/8 tsp mace

FOR THE GLAZE

225 ml/8 fl oz guava or other fruit purée
  such as mango or plum
3 Tbsp clear honey
3 Tbsp orange juice
2 Tbsp soy sauce
2 Tbsp fresh lime juice
1 tsp ground ginger
1/2 tsp ground allspice
1 tsp sea salt
1/2 tsp white pepper

4 racks baby back pork spare ribs (450 to
  900 g/1 to 2 lb each)

Make the rub. Combine the brown sugar, granulated sugar, seasoned salt, garlic salt, celery salt, chilli powder, pepper, allspice, ginger, cayenne, cloves and mace in a bowl and blend well. Place in an airtight container. Set aside until ready to use.

For the glaze, combine the fruit purée, honey, orange juice, soy sauce, lime juice, ginger, allspice, salt and pepper in a saucepan and heat over medium-low heat, stirring with a wire whisk. Heat for about 10 minutes until the sauce is well incorporated. Set aside and keep warm.

Remove the membrane from the back of the spare ribs. Sprinkle both sides of each rack of ribs with the rub. Place on your pit and cook indirectly for 4 to 6 hours, turning after 2 hours then again 1 hour later. To test if the ribs are cooked take two ribs side by side and see if they tear apart easily. If they are almost ready coat each slab on both sides with the glaze, using a pastry brush, then cook for 10 to 15 minutes and repeat the process. Remove the spare ribs from your cooker and leave them to rest for 10 to 15 minutes. Cut into serving pieces.

JAMAICAN JERKED PORK TENDERLOIN

Serves 6 to 8

FOR THE WET JERK RUB

1 bunch spring onions,
   cut into 2.5-cm/1-in pieces
3 Tbsp fresh thyme leaves
3 Tbsp grated root ginger
2 Tbsp fresh lime juice
1 Tbsp ground coriander
1 Tbsp ground black pepper
5 large cloves garlic, crushed
2 hot chillies, seeded and halved
2 tsp sea salt
2 tsp ground allspice
1 tsp ground nutmeg
1 tsp ground cinnamon
$\frac{1}{2}$ tsp powdered bay leaf
3 Tbsp groundnut oil

Four 450-g/1-lb pork tenderloins,
   trimmed of membrane and fat

Because this rub calls for hot chillies, so wear rubber gloves while preparing it. Combine the spring onions, thyme, ginger, lime juice, coriander, pepper, garlic, hot chillies, salt, allspice, nutmeg, cinnamon and bay leaf in a blender fitted with a steel blade and process until smooth. Add the oil in a thin stream while processing, until it is all incorporated.

Divide the jerk mixture in half. Place the tenderloins in a glass baking dish and, wearing rubber gloves, rub all over with the mixture. Cover and marinate for 4 hours in the refrigerator. Remove from the marinade and smoke-roast for about 2 hours or until the internal temperature reaches 62 to 71°C/145 to 160°F. Baste with the reserved marinade every 30 minutes. This dish is good served with rice and beans, and chilli sauce.

GLAZED VEAL RIBLETS

Serves 6 to 8

FOR THE MARINADE AND GLAZE

225 ml/8 fl oz fresh lemon juice
225 ml/8 fl oz honey
4 spring onions, thinly sliced
3 Tbsp hoisin sauce
3 Tbsp sesame oil
3 Tbsp pineapple juice
2 Tbsp grated root ginger
2 Tbsp crushed garlic
1 Tbsp grated lemon rind
1 tsp sea salt

2.7 kg/6 lb veal riblets, 6 cm/2½ in
   long, cut into 2-rib sections and
   trimmed

Combine the lemon juice, honey, spring onions, hoisin sauce, sesame oil, pineapple juice, ginger, garlic, lemon rind and salt in a bowl and blend well with a wire whisk to emulsify. Pour the marinade over the riblets, turning to coat well. Cover and marinate for 4 to 6 hours in the refrigerator. Remove the veal from the marinade, reserving it to use as a glaze. Place on your cooker and cook for 4 to 5 hours or until the ribs tear easily, brushing with the glaze 15 minutes before they are ready.

Jamaican Jerked Pork Tenderloin

MEMPHIS-STYLE PORK LOIN
WITH BARBECUE SAUCE

Serves 8 to 10

FOR THE MEMPHIS
BARBECUE RUB

2 Tbsp sea salt
1 Tbsp light brown sugar
1 tsp grated lemon rind
1 tsp finely ground black pepper
1 tsp cayenne
1 tsp chilli powder
1 tsp mustard powder
1 tsp garlic powder
½ tsp ground cinnamon

One 1.4- to 1.8-kg/3- to 4-lb
boneless pork loin, trimmed
100 ml/4 fl oz yellow mustard

FOR THE MEMPHIS
BASTING SAUCE

225 ml/8 fl oz cider or red wine
vinegar
225 ml/8 fl oz water or stock

Barbecue sauce

450 ml/16 fl oz ketchup
225 ml/8 fl oz cider vinegar
125 g/4 oz butter
125 g/4 oz dark brown sugar
3 Tbsp mustard powder
3 Tbsp Worcestershire sauce
1 tsp Tabasco sauce
3 whole lemons

To make the rub combine the salt, sugar, lemon rind, pepper, cayenne, chilli powder, dry mustard, garlic and cinnamon in a bowl and blend well. Store in an airtight container in a cool dark place.

Rub or paint the pork loin all over with the mustard using a pastry brush. Season all over with the rub. Place on your cooker and smoke for 3 to 5 hours or until the internal temperature is 62 to 71°C/145 to 160°F.

Combine the ingredients for the basting sauce and use to baste the pork after 1½ hours; baste every 30 to 45 minutes. If preferred, apple juice or cider can replace the basting sauce. During the last 30 to 45 minutes, glaze, using 225 ml/8 fl oz of the barbecue sauce.

To make the barbecue sauce combine the ketchup, vinegar, butter, sugar, mustard, Worcestershire sauce, Tabasco sauce and lemons in a saucepan over medium heat. Squeeze the juice out of the lemons into the sauce through a sieve, to remove the seeds and add the pulp and rind to the mixture. Bring to the boil, stirring with a wire whisk. Reduce the heat and simmer for 30 minutes. Remove the lemons before serving.

ROSEMARY AND GARLIC ROAST PORK
WITH BALSAMIC RHUBARB COMPOTE

Serves 4 to 6

FOR THE DIJON MUSTARD
SLATHER

3 Tbsp Dijon mustard
2 Tbsp flat beer
2 tsp brown sugar
½ tsp hot chilli sauce
½ tsp salt
½ tsp freshly ground black pepper

One 2- to 2.3-kg/4½- to 5-lb pork
   loin on the bone, trimmed
4 large cloves garlic, thinly sliced
2 Tbsp fresh rosemary leaves

Combine the mustard, beer, brown sugar, hot sauce, salt and pepper and blend well. Cover and set aside. With a sharp-pointed paring knife cut slits about 2.5 centimetres/1 inch apart in the fat of the meat and insert a sliver of garlic in the cuts. With a pastry brush, paint the roast with the mustard slather and sprinkle it with the rosemary leaves.

Place the roast in your smoker and smoke for about 3 hours at 105 to 120°C/230 to 250°F or until the internal temperature is 62 to 71°C/145 to 160°F. Leave to rest for about 15 minutes, slice, and serve with balsamic rhubarb compote.

Balsamic rhubarb compote

225 g/8 oz granulated sugar
225 ml/8 fl oz water
3 Tbsp balsamic vinegar
1 tsp grated root ginger
½ tsp sea salt
225 g/8 oz diced fresh rhubarb

Combine the sugar, water, vinegar, ginger and salt in a saucepan and bring to the boil, stirring to dissolve the sugar and salt. Stir in the rhubarb and simmer until tender but still crisp, 1 to 2 minutes. Transfer the rhubarb with a slotted spoon to a bowl. Simmer the sugar water until it has thickened. Remove from the heat and stir in the rhubarb. Serve the compote warm or at room temperature.

LIME AND GARLIC PORK TENDERLOIN
WITH JALAPEÑO ONION MARMALADE

Serves 4

FOR THE MARINADE

3 Tbsp fresh lime juice
4 cloves garlic, chopped
2 Tbsp soy sauce
2 Tbsp grated root ginger
1 Tbsp Dijon mustard
1 tsp sea salt
$\frac{1}{2}$ tsp freshly ground black pepper
$\frac{1}{2}$ tsp cayenne
$\frac{1}{2}$ cup olive oil

Four 350-g/12-oz pork tenderloins, trimmed

Combine the lime juice, garlic, soy sauce, ginger, mustard, salt, pepper, cayenne and oil in a blender or food processor fitted with a steel blade. Process until well blended, about 1 to 2 minutes.

Place the tenderloins in a glass baking dish or in a zip-lock type plastic bag; pour the marinade over the tenderloins and cover or seal. Marinate for 4 to 5 hours in the refrigerator or overnight.

Remove the pork from the marinade, reserving the marinade, and place on your smoker. Smoke for $1\frac{1}{2}$ to 2 hours or until the internal temperature reaches 62 to 71°C/145 to 160°F. Leave to rest for 10 to 15 minutes, slice, and serve warm with jalapeño onion marmalade and a salad of your choice.

Jalapeño onion marmalade

3 red onions, diced
3 Tbsp sunflower oil
1 tsp sea salt
1 tsp freshly ground black pepper
2 fresh red jalapeño chillies, seeded and chopped
2 Tbsp granulated sugar
3 Tbsp red wine vinegar
3 Tbsp water

In a large frying pan sauté the onions in the oil, with salt and pepper, over medium heat until soft, stirring occasionally. Add the jalapeño chillies and cook for 1 minute, stirring. Add the sugar, stirring until dissolved. Add the vinegar and simmer, stirring until almost all the liquid is evaporated. Add the water and simmer, stirring until the mixture is slightly thickened and the onions are very tender, about 8 to 10 minutes. Serve hot or at room temperature.

PORK TENDERLOIN WITH CAJUN CRAB, PRAWN AND CHEDDAR CHEESE STUFFING

Serves 6 to 8

2 pork tenderloins (900 g to 1.8 kg/
    2 to 4 lb), trimmed of membrane
    and fat

FOR THE STUFFING

1 tsp sea salt
1 tsp white pepper
½ tsp finely ground black pepper
½ tsp cayenne
¼ tsp fresh thyme leaves
¼ tsp fresh oregano leaves
125 g/4 oz butter
1 onion, chopped
1 small stalk celery, chopped
4 large cloves garlic, crushed
½ sweet red pepper, chopped
6 spring onions, very thinly sliced
225 g/8 oz fresh, frozen or canned
    crab meat, picked over
225 g/8 oz fresh prawns, peeled,
    deveined and chopped
3 Tbsp dry vermouth
175 g/6 oz very fine dried
    breadcrumbs
50 g/2 oz unsalted butter
1 large egg
50 g/2 oz grated Cheddar cheese or
    125 g/4 oz grated Parmesan

FOR THE LEMON BUTTER
BASTE

125 g/4 oz butter, melted
2 Tbsp fresh lemon juice

Flatten the tenderloins by placing them between two pieces of greaseproof paper or clingfilm and pounding them with a meat mallet. Cover and set aside in the refrigerator.

Combine the salt, white pepper, black pepper, cayenne, thyme and oregano in a small bowl and blend well.

Place half the butter in a large non-stick frying pan over medium-high heat, add the onions, celery, garlic and red pepper and sauté until soft, about 4 to 5 minutes. Add the seasoning and blend well. Add the rest of the butter and the spring onions and sauté for about 3 minutes or until the butter is melted and hot. Add the crab and prawns and sauté until just cooked, pour in the vermouth and sauté, stirring until the liquid has reduced by half. Stir in 80 g/3 oz breadcrumbs and cook, without stirring, until the mixture sticks, about 1 minute. Stir and scrape the bottom of the pan, then add the butter and continue cooking until the butter melts, stirring and scraping the pan bottom continuously. Stir in the remaining breadcrumbs and remove from the heat; cool slightly. Combine the egg with the cheese, add to the stuffing and blend well. Transfer the stuffing to a shallow baking dish and refrigerate until well chilled.

Lay the flattened tenderloins on your worktop and divide the filling between the tenderloins. Spread out the stuffing to within 2.5 centimetres/ 1 inch inside the meat and roll up like Swiss rolls. Place on your cooker and smoke for 2 to 3 hours or until the internal temperature is 71°C/160°F, basting with the lemon butter baste every 45 minutes as it cooks.

To make the lemon butter baste, melt 125 g/4 oz butter with the lemon juice in a small saucepan over medium heat then leave to rest for about 10 to 15 minutes. Slice and serve warm, with your favourite barbecue sauce on the side.

CAJUN RIB ROAST WITH SWEET PEPPER AND HOT CHILLI SAUCE

Serves 12 to 15

FOR THE CAJUN
SEASONING

1 Tbsp paprika
1 Tbsp cayenne
2 tsp mustard powder
2 tsp seasoned salt
1 tsp finely ground black pepper
1 tsp garlic powder
1 tsp ground sage
$\frac{1}{2}$ tsp white pepper
$\frac{1}{2}$ tsp onion powder
$\frac{1}{2}$ tsp ground cumin
$\frac{1}{2}$ tsp ground thyme
$\frac{1}{2}$ tsp ground oregano
$\frac{1}{2}$ tsp ground marjoram

One 8.2-kg/18-lb rib of beef,
   on the bone
10 large cloves garlic, sliced
   into slivers

FOR THE SAUCE

3 Tbsp olive oil
4 cloves garlic, crushed
1 red pepper, seeded, ribs removed
   and cut into thin strips
1 green pepper, seeded, ribs
   removed and cut into thin strips
1 yellow pepper, seeded, ribs
   removed and cut into thin strips
2 jalapeño chillies, seeded, ribs
   removed and cut into thin strips
2 Serrano chillies, seeded, ribs
   removed and cut into thin strips
225 ml/8 fl oz Marsala
1 l/1¾ pt brown sauce

Combine the paprika, cayenne, mustard, seasoned salt, black pepper, garlic, sage, white pepper, onion, cumin, thyme, oregano and marjoram, blending well. Set aside.

Remove the fat and thick membrane from the back of the ribs. Using a sharp pointed knife, outline the bones with the knifepoint, penetrating about 2.5 centimetres/1 inch. Pull back the flap that covers the meat but leave it attached.

Using a thin sharp knife, puncture the meat all over, making about 40 slits, and insert a sliver of garlic into each. Rub the Cajun seasoning all over the meat. Replace the flap, place in your cooker and smoke for 4 to 6 hours or to an internal temperature of 54°C/130°F for medium-rare, or longer if preferred.

While the meat is cooking, make the sauce. Heat the oil in a heavy saucepan and sauté the garlic and chillies. Cook until soft. Blot away any excess oil with kitchen paper. Deglaze the pan with the Marsala and, over medium-low heat, carefully ignite to burn off the alcohol. Reduce the wine to a glaze. Add the brown sauce. Cook the sauce until reduced to a consistency that will coat the back of a spoon. Strain the sauce into a container and chill until ready to serve. Remove the roast and allow to stand for 30 minutes. Serve sliced with the sauce.

Remove any fat that forms on top of the sauce. Serve hot, spooned over the meat.

Festive Ham with Fruit and Nut Stuffing

Serves 8 to 10

Half a fresh ham, 2.3 to 2.7 kg/5 to 6 lb, boned and flattened

FOR THE MARINADE

450 ml/16 fl oz dry white wine
450 ml/16 fl oz apple juice
100 ml/4 fl oz cider vinegar
100 ml/4 fl oz Calvados
½ onion, chopped
3 Tbsp brown sugar
1 Tbsp grated root ginger
1 Tbsp whole allspice, crushed
1 Tbsp peppercorns, crushed
4 cloves garlic, crushed
5 whole cloves
2 whole cinnamon sticks
½ tsp cardamom seeds, crushed

FOR THE STUFFING

50 g/2 oz unsalted butter
2 bunches spring onions, chopped
4 large cloves garlic, crushed
175 g/6 oz dried apricots
50 g/2 oz pistachio nuts, shelled
50 g/2 oz pine nuts, roasted
6 Tbsp chopped fresh parsley
2 Tbsp grated lemon rind
1 Tbsp balsamic vinegar
1 Tbsp brown sugar
1 tsp freshly ground black pepper

Combine the wine, apple juice, vinegar, Calvados, onion, ginger, sugar, allspice, peppercorns, garlic, cloves, cinnamon and cardamom in a non-reactive bowl and blend well. Place the ham in a non-reactive baking dish or a zip-lock type plastic bag. Place in the refrigerator and marinate for 2 days, turning every 12 hours.

To make the stuffing melt the butter in a large frying pan over medium-high heat. Add the spring onions and garlic and sauté for 3 to 4 minutes. Remove from the heat and add the apricots, pistachio nuts, pine nuts, parsley, lemon rind, vinegar, sugar and pepper, blending well. Place in a container, cover and refrigerate for 2 days.

Remove the ham from the marinade and pat dry, using kitchen paper. Strain the marinade and set aside.

You can either stuff the ham or cook the stuffing separately. Spread the stuffing mixture over the inside of the ham to within 2.5 centimetres/1 inch of the edges. Roll and tie together every 5 centimetres/2 inches. If the skin is intact score it into a diamond pattern using a sharp knife. Place in the cooker and smoke until the internal temperature is 71°C/160°F, about 8 hours.

To cook the stuffing separately, place the mixture in a roasting tin and top it with the flattened ham; you may have to cut it in half. Place it skin-side up, inside the edges and cut a 2.5- x 2.5-centimetre/1- x 1-inch diamond pattern. Place in the cooker and smoke until the internal temperature reaches 71°C/160°F. The cooking time will be 5 to 6 hours. Baste with the reserved marinade every hour.

CHILLI-RUBBED RACK OF LAMB WITH PUMPKIN SEED SAUCE

Serves 2

3 Tbsp chilli powder
1 Tbsp roasted ground cumin
1 Tbsp sugar
2 tsp garlic powder
1 tsp dried oregano
1 tsp sea salt
1 tsp freshly ground black pepper
2 racks spring lamb, trimmed

FOR THE SAUCE

3 Tbsp fresh coriander
3 Tbsp fresh mint leaves
2 shallots, diced
2 Tbsp raw pumpkin seeds
1 Serrano chilli, chopped
2 Tbsp fresh lime juice
2 Tbsp water
2 Tbsp groundnut oil
1 Tbsp sugar
1 tsp sea salt

Combine the chilli powder, cumin, sugar, garlic, oregano, salt and pepper in a bowl and blend well.

Season each rack of lamb with the chilli seasoning and rub into the meat. Cover the racks and leave to rest for 1 hour at room temperature or overnight in the refrigerator.

Combine the coriander, mint, shallots, pumpkin seeds, Serrano chilli, lime juice, water, oil, sugar and salt in a blender fitted with a steel blade. Purée until smooth, about 3 to 4 minutes.

Place the lamb on your smoke-roaster and smoke for about 2 hours or until the internal temperature reaches 54°C/130°F for medium-rare, or longer if preferred. Serve with pumpkin seed sauce and roasted red onions, if you like.

Calf's Liver with Melon, Madeira and Ham

Serves 8 to 10

1 honeydew or Cantaloupe melon
350 ml/12 fl oz Madeira
2 Tbsp cracked black pepper
1 Tbsp coarse salt
1.8 kg/4 lb calf's liver, cleaned, rolled
   and tied
3 Tbsp mustard slather
   (see page 61)
6 to 8 rashers bacon
6 shallots, chopped
3 Tbsp balsamic vinegar
450 ml/16 fl oz beef or chicken stock
125 g/4 oz unsalted butter, cubed and
   chilled
2 Tbsp chopped fresh chives
225 g/8 oz ham, rind removed, thinly
   sliced and diced

Spoon out some flesh from the melon and make a round indentation large enough to scrape or shake out the seeds. Pour some Madeira into the hole, replace the melon flesh on top and chill overnight in the refrigerator.

Coat the liver all over with mustard slather, season with the salt and pepper and lay the bacon rashers on top. Place on the smoker, using apple wood. Smoke for 1 to 2 hours or until the internal temperature is between 50 and 54°C/120 and 130°F.

Remove the 'plug' from the melon indentation, and pour the Madeira into a bowl and reserve. Peel and slice the melon. Cut into medium-sized chunks and put into a bowl. Pour a small amount of the reserved Madeira over the melon, cover, set aside and keep cool.

Place the shallots and vinegar in a saucepan over medium heat. Reduce by three-quarters, add the remaining reserved Madeira and reduce to 3 tablespoons. Add the stock and reduce to about 350 ml/12 fl oz. Reduce the heat to a low simmer. Adjust the seasoning. Set aside and keep warm.

To serve, remove the strings and bacon from the liver. Slice into 5-millimetre/ ¼-inch slices; place on a serving platter or plates. Whisk the butter into the sauce until incorporated, pour the sauce over the meat and garnish with melon, chopped chives and diced ham.

Beef Brisket with Spicy Barbecue Rub and Angel's Mustard Slather

Serves 8 to 10

One 1.8 to 3.6-kg/4 to 8-lb beef brisket

FOR THE SPICY BARBECUE RUB

3 Tbsp granulated sugar
1 Tbsp garlic salt
1 Tbsp celery salt
1 Tbsp barbecue spice
2 Tbsp paprika
1 Tbsp chilli powder
1 Tbsp finely ground black pepper
1 tsp celery seeds
$\frac{1}{2}$ tsp cayenne
$\frac{1}{4}$ tsp ground cloves

FOR THE ANGEL'S MUSTARD SLATHER

2 tsp garlic powder
1 tsp onion powder
1 tsp finely ground black pepper
$\frac{1}{2}$ tsp cayenne
$\frac{1}{2}$ tsp white pepper
$\frac{1}{2}$ tsp sea salt
2 Tbsp soy sauce
2 Tbsp white wine
2 Tbsp Worcestershire sauce
225 g/8 oz Dijon mustard

Trim the fat from the brisket leaving a 3- to 5-millimetre/$\frac{1}{8}$- to $\frac{1}{4}$-inch fat cap. Trim the fat pockets even with the side of the brisket. Cover and set aside.

For the rub, combine the sugar, garlic salt, celery salt, barbecue spice, paprika, chilli powder, black pepper, celery seeds, cayenne and cloves and blend well. Store in an airtight container in a cool dry place.

To make the angel's mustard slather, add the garlic, onion, peppers and salt to a non-reactive bowl. Blend in the soy sauce, white wine, and Worcestershire sauce and dissolve the spices with a wire whisk. Stir in the mustard and incorporate all the ingredients.

Using a pastry brush, cover the lean side of the meat with the mustard slather. Season with the rub, sprinkle on salt and pepper and do not rub in. Turn the brisket and repeat the process on the fat side. Place on your cooker and smoke for 8 to 12 hours or until a skewer inserted in the flat part of the brisket, against the grain, goes in easily and comes out with no resistance.

Beef Tenderloin
with Raspberry Ginger Sauce and Garlic Mashed Potatoes

Serves 8 to 10

FOR THE SEASONING

3 Tbsp dried brown sugar
2 Tbsp garlic salt
2 Tbsp onion salt
2 Tbsp paprika
1 Tbsp chilli powder
1 Tbsp black pepper
1 tsp cayenne
$\frac{1}{2}$ tsp dried oregano
$\frac{1}{2}$ tsp ground ginger
$\frac{1}{2}$ tsp ground coriander
$\frac{1}{4}$ tsp celery seeds

One 1.8 to 2.3-kg/4 to 5-lb beef-tenderloin,
**   trimmed of membrane and fat**
3 Tbsp olive oil

Combine the sugar, garlic salt, onion salt, paprika, chilli powder, pepper, cayenne, oregano, ginger, coriander and celery seeds in a bowl and mix well. Store in an airtight container in a cool dry place.

Rub the trimmed tenderloin all over with the olive oil and season all over with the beef seasoning. Place on your cooker and smoke with fruitwood for 1 to 3 hours or until the tenderloin reaches 54°C/130°F for medium-rare, or longer if preferred.

Raspberry ginger sauce

450 ml/16 fl oz ketchup	2 Tbsp Worcestershire sauce
3 Tbsp grated root ginger	2 Tbsp soy sauce
4 cloves garlic, crushed	2 Tbsp cider vinegar
350 ml/12 fl oz Melba sauce	1 Tbsp grated orange rind
(raspberry sauce)	2 spring onions, chopped
3 Tbsp brown sugar	1 tsp ground allspice
3 Tbsp clear honey	1 tsp sea salt
3 Tbsp fresh orange juice	
2 Tbsp Grand Marnier or	
Cointreau	

While the meat is cooking make the sauce. Combine the ketchup, ginger, garlic, Melba sauce, sugar, honey, orange juice, Grand Marnier or Cointreau, Worcestershire sauce, soy sauce, vinegar, orange rind, spring onions, allspice and salt in a saucepan and bring to the boil, stirring constantly. Reduce the heat and simmer, stirring occasionally, for 30 minutes. Strain and discard the spring onions. Serve hot.

Serve the meat with the raspberry ginger sauce on the side and accompany with garlic mashed potatoes.

Garlic mashed potatoes

4 whole heads garlic, tops removed
100 ml/4 fl oz olive oil
2.3 kg/5 lb floury potatoes
1 Tbsp sea salt
125 g/4 oz butter
450 ml/16 fl oz warm milk
1 tsp sea salt
$^1/_2$ tsp white pepper

Pour the olive oil over the cut part of the garlic heads. Place on your smoker for about 2 hours or until the cloves are soft and tender. Remove the cloves from their skin, set aside 6 to 8 for the mashed potatoes, place the rest in a sterile jar, cover with a layer of olive oil, seal and refrigerate. This smoke-roasted garlic will last for about 1 week in the refrigerator.

Wash the potatoes, place in a large pot and cover with cold water and 1 tablespoon sea salt. Bring to the boil. Reduce the heat and simmer until tender. Drain the potatoes and place in a bowl. Add the reserved cloves of smoke-roasted garlic, butter, and warm milk and mash to the desired texture. Season to taste.

Pastrami with Irish Whiskey Sauce

Serves 6 to 8

One 1.8-kg/4-lb brisket or boned rib roast

FOR THE BRINING OR CURE

225 g/8 oz sea salt
125 g/4 oz granulated sugar
3 Tbsp meat tenderizer
1.8 l/3¼ pt water
2 Tbsp pickling spice
2 tsp whole black peppercorns
2 bay leaves, crumbled
2 cloves garlic, crushed
125 to 175 g/4 to 6 oz coarsely ground black pepper
125 g/4 oz coarsely ground coriander

FOR THE SAUCE

225 g/8 oz Irish whiskey
300 g/10 oz dark brown sugar
3 Tbsp Dijon mustard
175 ml/6 fl oz apple juice
1 tsp sea salt
1 Tbsp arrowroot
2 Tbsp cold water

Start brining the meat seven days before you intend to smoke it. Combine the salt, sugar, meat tenderizer, water, pickling spice, peppercorns, bay leaf and garlic, in a large non-reactive bowl or stockpot. Place the beef in the brine and weigh it down, making sure that it is always submerged. Cover and refrigerate for seven days. Turn the beef at least once a day. Remove the beef from the brine and rinse with cold water.

Combine the pepper and coriander in a small bowl and blend well. Press the pepper-coriander mixture into the beef. Place the beef on your cooker and smoke for 4 to 10 hours or until a skewer can be inserted easily against the grain and comes out easily. The reason for the large variance in time is because if you use a boned rib roast it could be ready 4 hours, whereas brisket can take 7 to 10 hours.

In a saucepan combine the whiskey, brown sugar, apple juice and salt over medium heat and simmer, stirring with a wire whisk. In a small bowl combine the arrowroot and cold water and blend into a paste. Stir in the sauce, stirring until thickened. Serve the sauce hot.

SMOKED LAMB
WITH RED PEPPER RELISH

Serves 6 to 8

One 3.2- to 4.1-kg/7- to 9-lb leg of lamb, trimmed

FOR THE MARINADE

2 medium onions, chopped
225 ml/8 fl oz red wine
125 ml/4 fl oz clear honey
3 Tbsp Worcestershire sauce
3 Tbsp sunflower oil
8 cloves garlic, chopped
1 tsp sea salt
1 tsp black pepper

Combine the onions, wine, honey, Worcestershire sauce, oil, garlic, salt and pepper in a blender fitted with a steel blade. Purée until smooth. Place the lamb in a zip-lock type plastic bag. Pour the marinade over it and seal. Marinate for 7 to 8 hours in the refrigerator or overnight.

To cook, remove the lamb from the marinade and smoke for about 4 hours or until the internal temperature reaches 54°C/130°F for medium-rare, or longer if preferred. Leave to rest for 10 to 15 minutes. Carve and serve with red pepper relish.

Red pepper relish

4 large sweet red peppers, diced
2 large red onions, diced
450 ml/16 fl oz cider vinegar
225 g/8 oz sugar
1 Tbsp hot red pepper flakes
2 tsp yellow mustard seeds
2 tsp sea salt

Put the peppers, onions, vinegar, sugar, hot red pepper flakes, mustard seeds and salt in a heavy saucepan over medium heat. Simmer, stirring occasionally, about 1 hour or until the mixture has reduced to about 700 ml/1¹/₄ pt. Serve the relish chilled or at room temperature.

Smoked Lamb with Red Pepper Relish

Venison with Wild Mushroom Sauce

Serves 6 to 8

3 Tbsp bacon dripping

2 Tbsp mustard powder

4 large cloves smoke-roasted garlic
(see page 73), crushed

2 tsp coarsely ground black pepper

1 tsp coarse salt

One 1.8-kg/4-lb loin of venison

FOR THE SAUCE

125 g/4 oz dried porcini mushrooms

1.8 l/3¼ pt water

225 ml/8 fl oz Madeira

225 g/8 oz unsalted butter, half of
which cut into cubes and freeze

450 g/1 lb assorted fresh, wild and
cultivated mushrooms, stemmed
and thinly sliced

3 to 5 Tbsp tomato purée

1 tsp sea salt

1 tsp freshly ground black pepper

Combine the bacon dripping, mustard, garlic, pepper and salt in a small bowl, blending well with a wire whisk. Rub the mixture all over the venison, wrap in clingfilm or place in a non-reactive baking dish, cover and marinate overnight in the refrigerator. Place on the cooker and smoke at least 121°C/250°F for 2 to 3 hours. Do not overcook: venison is usually served rare or medium-rare.

In a large saucepan, combine the dried mushrooms and the water. Cook over high heat for 30 to 35 minutes. Strain through muslin and squeeze the liquid from the mushrooms to extract all the juice and flavour. Discard the mushrooms and return the broth to the pan. Add the Madeira and bring to the boil. Reduce to 350 to 450 ml/12 to 16 fl oz.

Melt the unfrozen 125 g/4 oz butter in a frying pan over medium heat and sauté the fresh mushrooms until tender, about 5 minutes. Set aside.

Over medium heat, add the tomato purée to the reduced mushroom liquid and blend with a wire whisk until smooth. Blend in the frozen butter cubes over low heat until they are all incorporated. Add the sautéed mushrooms, salt and pepper. Set aside and keep warm.

Slice the venison into medallions and top with a little sauce. Serve the remaining sauce on the side.

Smoked Black Bean Duck
with Spicy Lo-mein

Serves 2 to 4

One 1.6- to 2-kg/3½- to 4½-lb
  duckling
100 ml/4 fl oz soy sauce
3 Tbsp fermented black beans,
  crushed
3 Tbsp dark brown sugar
4 cloves garlic, crushed
2 tsp ground cinnamon
½ tsp Chinese five-spice powder
3 spring onions, diced

FOR THE MARINADE
AND BASTE

225 ml/8 fl oz soy sauce
1 Tbsp granulated sugar
2 tsp grated root ginger
1 tsp garlic, crushed

Wash and rinse the duck, and pat dry with kitchen paper. Tie the neck with string, or secure with skewers to seal it. Combine the soy sauce, black beans, sugar, garlic, cinnamon, five-spice powder and spring onions in a bowl and blend well. Pour into the body cavity of the duck. Insert skewers across the opening and lace tightly with string to prevent the sauce from oozing out.

For the marinade, combine the soy sauce, sugar, ginger and garlic in a bowl and blend well with a wire whisk.

Place the duck in a heavy-duty plastic bag and pour the marinade over. Press all the air out of the bag and tie it with string. Marinate the duck in the refrigerator for 3 to 4 hours or overnight.

Remove the duck from the marinade, reserving it to use as a baste. Place the duck on your cooker and smoke for 2 to 3 hours at 121°C/250°F, basting the duck about every 30 minutes with the reserved marinade. If you prefer your duck rare reduce the cooking time by half.

Spicy lo-mein

Serves 4 to 6

3 Tbsp groundnut oil
3 cloves garlic, crushed
1 Tbsp grated root ginger
1 to 2 tsp crushed red peppers
2 spring onions, cut on a bias
50 g/2 oz bamboo shoots, sliced
1 small celery stalk, sliced
3 Tbsp chopped onion
50 g/2 oz sliced mushrooms
50 g/2 oz bean sprouts
250 g/8 oz noodles, such as linguine
  or spaghetti, cooked
3 Tbsp soy sauce
1 Tbsp granulated sugar
1 Tbsp sherry
2 tsp sesame oil
1 tsp freshly ground black pepper
½ tsp sea salt

Add the groundnut oil to a large frying pan or wok and heat until almost smoking. Add the garlic, ginger and crushed red peppers and sauté or stir-fry for about 1 minute until fragrant. Combine the spring onions, bamboo shoots, celery, onions and mushrooms; add to the wok or frying pan and stir-fry for 2 to 3 minutes. Add the bean sprouts and cook for about 1 minute. Add the noodles and cook for 1 to 2 minutes or until warm. Combine the soy sauce, sherry, sesame oil, pepper and salt and add to the vegetable-noodle mixture and toss to blend.

BEER-MARINATED CHICKEN

Serves 4 to 8

FOR THE BEER MARINADE

450 ml/16 fl oz bottled Italian
   salad dressing
350 ml/12 oz flat beer from
   2 cans of beer, reserving
   $\frac{1}{2}$ of each beer
4 large cloves garlic, crushed
2 Tbsp grated onions
2 Tbsp granulated sugar
1 Tbsp coarsely ground
   black pepper
2 tsp coarse salt
1 tsp grated lemon rind
1 tsp fresh tarragon leaves

2 whole 1.4- to 1.8-kg/3- to 4-lb
   chickens

FOR THE SPICY
BARBECUED
CHICKEN RUB

125 g/4 oz granulated sugar
5 Tbsp celery salt
5 Tbsp onion salt
2 Tbsp garlic salt
5 Tbsp paprika
1 Tbsp chilli powder
2 tsp grated lemon rind
2 tsp finely ground black pepper
1 to 2 tsp cayenne
1 tsp rubbed sage
1 tsp dried basil
1 tsp dried tarragon

Combine the salad dressing, beer, garlic, onion, sugar, pepper, salt, lemon rind and tarragon in a bowl and blend well with a wire whisk.

Rinse the chicken with cold water; remove the giblets and reserve for another purpose or discard. Pat dry with kitchen paper. Place the chickens in a heavy plastic bag and pour the marinade over them, remove all of the air in the bag, and tie shut. Marinate the chickens for 4 hours in the refrigerator.

Combine the sugar, celery salt, onion salt, garlic salt, paprika, chilli powder, lemon rind, pepper, cayenne to taste, sage, basil and tarragon in a bowl and blend well.

Remove the chickens from the marinade, lightly pat dry with kitchen paper and season inside and out with the rub. Place the chicken on the upright half-full beer cans, positioning the legs out in front, and put in your cooker. Smoke-roast for about 4 hours or until the internal temperature is 71°C/160°F or until the juices run clear.

Beer-marinated Chicken

TANDOORI CHICKEN BREASTS

Serves 6

FOR THE MARINADE

¹⁄₈ tsp saffron threads
2 Tbsp boiling water
225 ml/8 fl oz plain yoghurt
2 Tbsp fresh lemon juice
2 Tbsp white wine vinegar
1 Tbsp paprika
2 tsp grated root ginger
3 cloves garlic, crushed
1 jalapeño chilli, seeded and finely chopped
1 tsp roasted ground cumin
1 tsp ground coriander
1 tsp curry powder
1 tsp cayenne
1 tsp salt
¹⁄₂ tsp ground cinnamon
¹⁄₂ tsp chilli powder

Six 150-g/5-oz boneless, skinless chicken breasts

Dissolve the saffron in a small bowl with the boiling water. Combine the yoghurt, lemon juice, vinegar, paprika, ginger, garlic, jalapeño chilli, cumin, coriander, curry powder, cayenne, salt, cinnamon and chilli powder in a non-reactive bowl and blend well with a wire whisk. Add the saffron and blend in.

Dip the chicken breasts into the marinade, covering on all sides, place in a glass baking dish, cover and marinate for 2 to 4 hours in the refrigerator. Place on your cooker and smoke for about 1 hour or until the internal temperature reaches 71°C/160°F. Serve with steamed rice.

Sweet and Spicy Poussins

Serves 8

4 poussins, halved

FOR THE MARINADE

900 g/2 lb tinned plums, drained
    and stoned
1 onion, diced
2 cloves garlic, crushed
3 Tbsp red wine
3 Tbsp teriyaki sauce
2 Tbsp chilli sauce
Juice of 1 lemon
2 tsp sesame oil
1 tsp salt
$\frac{1}{2}$ tsp black pepper

Rinse the poussins in cold water and pat dry with kitchen paper. Make several deep slashes in the flesh of each poussin half. Set aside. Place all the ingredients, except the poussin halves, in a food processor or blender. Process until smooth. Place the poussins cut-side down in a non-reactive dish. Pour over the marinade. Cover and marinate in the refrigerator, turning and basting frequently, for at least 24 hours. Drain the poussins, reserving the marinade. Place the poussins on your cooker and smoke for 3 to 4 hours or until the internal temperature is 71°C/160°F or the juices run clear.

Barbecued Chicken

Serves 6 to 8

FOR THE MARINADE

125 ml/4 fl oz sunflower oil
5 Tbsp soy sauce
3 Tbsp Worcestershire sauce
3 Tbsp red wine vinegar
2 Tbsp fresh lemon juice
1 Tbsp mustard powder
1 Tbsp chopped fresh parsley
1 tsp chopped fresh basil
2 large cloves garlic, crushed
1 tsp sea salt
1 tsp freshly ground black pepper

2 whole 1.8- to 2.3-kg/4- to 5-lb
    chickens

Combine the oil, soy sauce, Worcestershire sauce, vinegar, lemon juice, mustard, parsley, basil, garlic, salt and pepper in a non-reactive bowl and blend well with a wire whisk. Cut the chicken into portions. Place in a zip-lock type plastic bag and pour the marinade over it. Marinate for 2 to 4 hours. Remove the chicken from the marinade, reserving it. Place the chicken on your cooker and cook for 2 to 5 hours or until the internal temperature is 71°C/160°F. After $1\frac{1}{2}$ hours baste with the reserved marinade every 30 minutes.

Sweet and Spicy Poussins

SMOKED CHICKEN LIVERS

**Serves 8 as a main course,
15 to 20 as a starter**

FOR THE BARBECUE
SEASONING

**2 Tbsp brown sugar
2 Tbsp granulated sugar
1 Tbsp garlic salt
1 Tbsp seasoned salt
1 Tbsp celery salt
2 Tbsp paprika
1 Tbsp chilli powder
1 Tbsp black pepper
1 tsp grated lemon rind
$\frac{1}{2}$ tsp mustard powder
$\frac{1}{2}$ tsp ground ginger
$\frac{1}{4}$ tsp ground allspice
$\frac{1}{8}$ tsp mace**

**80 chicken livers
Non-stick cooking spray or olive oil**

Combine the brown sugar, sugar, garlic salt, seasoned salt, celery salt, paprika, chilli powder, black pepper, lemon rind, mustard, ginger, allspice and mace in a bowl and blend well. Store in an airtight container in a cool dry place.

Soak 8 wooden skewers in water for 30 minutes. Thread 10 livers on each skewer, coat with non-stick spray or oil and season to taste with the barbecue seasoning. Place on your smoker and smoke for about 1 hour, being careful not to overcook beyond 48°C/120°F if using a thermometer. Serve with your favourite salsa.

CAJUN-MARINATED TURKEY KEBABS

Serves 6 to 8

450 to 900 g/1 to 2 lb turkey fillets
    cut into 2.5-cm/1-in cubes
450 g/1 lb smoked or Polish
    Kielbasa sausage, cut into
    chunks
2 large sweet red peppers, seeded
    and cut into 2.5-cm/1-in pieces
1 large onion cut into 2.5-cm/1-in
    pieces

FOR THE MARINADE

225 ml/8 fl oz Dijon mustard
125 ml/4 fl oz fresh lemon juice
3 Tbsp Cajun seasoning
1 clove garlic, crushed
3 Tbsp white wine
3 Tbsp olive oil
1 Tbsp coarse salt

Combine all the ingredients in a bowl and blend well with a wire whisk. Cover and marinate the turkey overnight in the refrigerator.

Thread the turkey, sausage, pepper and onion onto 8 skewers. Place on the cooker and smoke for 2 to 3 hours until the internal temperature is 71°C/160°F.

CURRIED CHICKEN WITH COCONUT SAUCE

Serves 6

FOR THE CURRY RUB

3 Tbsp granulated sugar
2 Tbsp curry powder
1 Tbsp garlic salt
2 tsp roasted ground cumin
1 tsp finely ground black pepper
1 tsp ground turmeric
1 tsp cayenne
1/2 tsp ground cardamom

Six 150-g/5-oz boneless, skinless
    chicken breasts

FOR THE SAUCE

50 g/2 oz butter
1 large onion, diced
4 large cloves garlic, crushed
1 to 2 Serrano chillies, seeded and
    finely chopped
3 Tbsp chicken stock
225 ml/8 fl oz coconut milk
1 tsp sea salt

Combine the sugar, curry powder, salt, cumin, pepper, turmeric, cayenne and cardamom in a bowl and blend well. Store in an airtight container in a cool dark place.

Season the chicken breasts on all sides with the curry rub and place on a plate. Cover with clingfilm and marinate for 1 to 2 hours in the refrigerator. Place on your cooker and smoke for 1 to 2 hours or until the internal temperature is 71°C/160°F.

Melt the butter in a medium saucepan over medium-high heat and add the onions, garlic and chillies. Sauté, stirring, until soft, about 4 to 5 minutes. Add the stock and simmer for 2 minutes. Add the coconut milk and salt. Simmer for 5 minutes. Set aside and keep warm. Serve over the chicken.

MARINATED QUAIL WITH SALAD AND PAPAYA-CHILLI VINAIGRETTE

Serves 2 to 4

8 quail, dressed

FOR THE MARINADE

1 cup olive oil
1 tsp each turmeric and mild paprika
1 clove garlic, crushed
1 tsp sea salt
½ tsp white pepper
Assorted green salad leaves

FOR THE VINAIGRETTE

1 roasted Serrano chilli, peeled,
    seeded and finely chopped
1 small papaya, peeled, seeded and
    diced
225 ml/8 fl oz olive oil
3 Tbsp Champagne vinegar

Heat the olive oil in a small saucepan until warm. Add the garlic, salt and pepper and remove from the heat. Add the turmeric and paprika and leave to cool.

Place the quail in a non-reactive bowl or dish and pour the marinade over them, making sure all are coated. Cover and marinate for 1 to 3 hours in the refrigerator.

Remove the quail from the marinade; reserve the marinade to baste with. Place the quail on your cooker and smoke for 1 to 2 hours, until tender, basting with the reserved marinade.

To make the vinaigrette, combine the Serrano and papaya in a bowl and mix well. Place half of the chilli-papaya mixture in a bowl with the olive oil and vinegar and blend well. Reserve the other half of the mixture.

To serve, place 2 quail on a serving plate with salad topped with vinaigrette. Garnish with the rest of the chilli-papaya mixture.

SOUTHWESTERN ORANGE ROUGHY

Serves 4 to 6

125 ml/4 fl oz soured cream
100 g/3 oz cream cheese, softened
125 g/4 oz grated Cheddar cheese
1 Tbsp grated onion
1 Tbsp fresh lime juice
½ tsp roasted ground cumin
½ tsp garlic powder
½ tsp sea salt
¼ tsp white pepper
¼ tsp cayenne
900 g/2 lb orange roughy or
    snapper fillets, cut into serving
    portions
Paprika, coriander sprigs, sliced
    pickled jalapeño chillies to
    garnish

Combine the soured cream and cream cheese and blend until smooth. Add the Cheddar cheese, onion and lime juice and blend in until as smooth as possible. Blend in the cumin, garlic, salt, white pepper and cayenne until smooth. Spread the mixture evenly over the fillets and place on your cooker. Smoke for 30 to 45 minutes or until the fish flakes easily. Carefully remove the fillets with a spatula, being careful not to lose any of the cheese mixture on top. Garnish with paprika, coriander sprigs and slices of jalapeño chilli. Heat any leftover mixture in a small saucepan until soft and warm and serve on the side.

Marinated Quail

FIVE-PEPPER PHEASANT

Serves 4 to 6

FOR THE FIVE-PEPPER
SEASONING

2 Tbsp demerara sugar
1 Tbsp coarse salt
2 tsp coarsely ground Szechuan
    pepper
2 tsp coarsely ground black
    peppercorns
2 tsp coarsely ground pink
    peppercorns
2 tsp coarsely ground green
    peppercorns
2 tsp coarsely ground allspice
1 tsp coarsely ground white
    peppercorns

2 oranges, halved
2 young 1.6-kg/3½-lb pheasants,
    dressed
10 to 12 rashers bacon

Combine the sugar, salt, Szechuan pepper, black pepper, pink peppercorns, green peppercorns, allspice and white pepper in a small bowl and blend well.

Cut the oranges in half and rub over the outside of the pheasants. Season inside and out with the pepper seasoning. Place the orange halves inside the pheasants. Cover the breast and legs with the bacon. Place on the cooker and smoke at at least 121°C/250°F for 2 to 3 hours, until the internal temperature is 71°C/160°F or until the juices run clear. Baste the pheasants with apple juice as they cook.

SMOKED OYSTERS ROCKEFELLER

Serves 24

50 g/2 oz butter
2 spring onions, thinly sliced
2 large cloves garlic, crushed
300 g/10 oz frozen chopped
    spinach, defrosted and drained
1 Tbsp dry sherry
1 tsp sea salt
1 tsp freshly ground pepper
25 g/1 oz fine dried breadcrumbs
2 dozen oysters on the half shell,
    grained
2 Tbsp fresh lemon juice
Hot chilli sauce
4 rashers bacon, fried until crisp
    and crumbled
24 strips smoked, roasted red
    pepper

Heat the butter in a saucepan over medium-high heat, add the onions and garlic and sauté until tender, about 3 minutes. Stir in the spinach, sherry, salt, and pepper and cook for a further 3 minutes. Remove from the heat and stir in the breadcrumbs. Place each oyster on a bottling screw-top lid and top each with some lemon juice and hot sauce. Top with the spinach mixture and garnish with bacon and red pepper strips. Place in your cooker and smoke for 20 minutes to 1 hour.

Five-pepper Pheasant

Barbecued Trout
with Lemon Rice Stuffing

Serves 6 to 8

FOR THE WHITE WINE
MARINADE

350 ml/12 fl oz dry vermouth
125 ml/4 fl oz fresh lemon juice
125 ml/4 fl oz olive oil
$^1\!/_2$ onion, grated
4 large cloves garlic, crushed
1 Tbsp grated root ginger
1 Tbsp dill
1 Tbsp hot chilli sauce
1 tsp fresh thyme leaves, chopped
1 tsp sea salt
1 tsp finely ground black pepper

Two 900-g/2-lb rainbow or brown
trout

Combine the vermouth, lemon juice, olive oil, onion, garlic, ginger, dill, hot sauce, thyme, salt and pepper in a bowl and blend well with a wire whisk. With a sharp knife score both sides of the fish by making four or five evenly spaced slits about 2.5 to 5 centimetres/1 to 2 inches long and about 5 millimetres/$^1\!/_4$ inch deep. Place the fish in a non-reactive baking dish or plastic bag and pour the marinade over the fish. Cover and marinate for 2 hours in the refrigerator. Turn the fish every 30 minutes to coat well.

Place the fish upright on your cooker so the skewers will hold it up. With a pastry brush, cover with olive oil and season with the dill. Smoke-roast for 1 to 2 hours using apple or alder wood, basting with the marinade as you cook, until the fish flakes easily.

Lemon rice stuffing

100 g/3 oz freshly cooked rice,
cooled
2 spring onions (white and green),
thinly sliced
3 Tbsp chopped fresh parsley
$^1\!/_2$ lemon, seeded and chopped
(include the peel)
1 Tbsp grated lemon rind
3 Tbsp olive oil
2 Tbsp dill

For the stuffing combine the rice, spring onions, parsley, lemon and lemon rind and blend well. Remove the fish from the marinade, drain on kitchen paper, and pat dry. Strain the marinade, add 3 tablespoons to the stuffing, and blend well. Reserve the excess marinade. Lightly insert the stuffing into the fish cavities. Using 3 to 5 bamboo skewers per fish, skewer each fish cavity 2.5 centimetres/1 inch from the front opening, breast area and 2.5 centimetres/1 inch from the rear end, with another in the middle. Secure with a double length of string.

SMOKED TROUT WITH SEASONED COUSCOUS AND BALSAMIC SMOKE-ROASTED ONIONS

Serves 4

Two 900-g/2-lb rainbow or brown trout
125 ml/4 fl oz sunflower oil
2 Tbsp coarse salt
½ Tbsp black pepper
½ Tbsp grated lemon rind

Rub the fish all over, inside and out with the oil. Combine the salt, black pepper and lemon rind in a small bowl and blend well. Season the fish inside and out with the mixture. To place the fish on your cooker, turn the belly flaps out as the base and set the fish up. Smoke for 1 to 2 hours or until the fish flakes easily. To serve, spoon couscous on a serving platter, top with the fish and place the onions around the edge.

Seasoned couscous

1 Tbsp groundnut oil
6 spring onions (green and white), thinly sliced
2 cloves garlic, crushed
175 ml/6 fl oz water
1 Tbsp chicken-flavoured stock granules
100 g/3 oz couscous
1 Tbsp light soy sauce
3 tomatoes, peeled, seeded and chopped
1 Tbsp chopped fresh parsley
1 tsp freshly ground black pepper

Add the oil to a saucepan over medium heat and sauté the spring onions and garlic until tender, about 2 to 3 minutes. Add the water and stock and bring to the boil. Remove from the heat. Stir in the couscous and soy sauce, cover and leave to stand for 5 minutes. Stir in the tomatoes, parsley and pepper. Cover and set aside.

Balsamic smoked-roasted onions

3 Tbsp olive oil
3 Tbsp balsamic vinegar
3 Tbsp granulated sugar
2 Tbsp soy sauce
2 large red onions, cut into wedges

Combine the olive oil, balsamic vinegar, sugar and soy sauce in a large bowl and blend well with a wire whisk until the sugar dissolves. Add the onion wedges and toss to coat. Pour all the ingredients in a shallow 23 x 32.5-centimetre/9 x 13-inch baking dish and place on your cooker. Smoke-roast, stirring every 20 minutes, for 2 hours or until the onions are soft and coated with a thick glaze.

Swordfish with Herbs, Smoked Bacon and Red Wine Butter Sauce

Serves 6 to 8

1.4 kg/3 lb swordfish
225 g/8 oz unsmoked bacon, rind removed, cut into matchstick strips
6 Tbsp chopped fresh basil
3 Tbsp chopped fresh thyme
3 Tbsp chopped fresh chervil
3 Tbsp chopped fresh tarragon
3 Tbsp olive oil
5 cloves garlic, crushed
1 Tbsp coarse salt
1 Tbsp fresh coarsely ground black pepper

FOR THE SAUCE

2 shallots, chopped
1 Tbsp olive oil
125 ml/4 fl oz red wine vinegar
1 tsp cracked black pepper
1 bay leaf
225 ml/8 fl oz red wine
225 ml/8 fl oz double cream
225 g/8 oz unsalted butter, cut into small pieces and kept cold

Have your fishmonger cut an even-sized section of fresh boneless, skinless swordfish. Divide in half.

Sauté the bacon in a large frying pan until medium-rare. Remove and drain on kitchen paper. Sauté the herbs over high heat for about 1 minute to wilt. Remove from the heat and drain.

Using a larding needle or sharp knife, insert the bacon evenly over both sections of the swordfish. Rub the olive oil all over the fish then rub the garlic over the top of the flesh. Season with the salt and pepper and top with the wilted herbs. Place in your cooker and smoke with the wood of your choice, for 1 to 1½ hours or until the fish flakes easily.

In a medium saucepan, stew the shallots in 1 tablespoon olive oil. Add the vinegar, cracked black pepper, and bay leaf and reduce to about 3 tablespoons. Add the red wine and reduce to 3 tablespoons. Add the double cream and reduce until it thickens. Beat in the butter, bit by bit, until it is all incorporated and strain through muslin or sieve. Keep warm.

Cut the swordfish into serving pieces. Place some sauce on the serving plates, top with the fish and serve. Garnish with lemon or lime wedges if liked.

ACCOMPANIMENTS AND DESSERTS

ACCOMPANIMENTS AND side dishes are as important a feature of a meal as the main course. When I plan a meal around smoked meats, the menu will contain French, Italian or garlic bread. I like beans so I usually include either a hot bean dish or a cold bean salad. As a general rule I plan to serve at least four side dishes, not counting the bread, to go with my meal.

If I plan a dessert it is something light and fresh, such as chilled fresh fruit, sorbet or maybe ice cream. If you have a favourite dish, you can experiement with the best smoked meats to complement it.

TABBOULEH

Serves 6 to 8

125 g/4 oz bulghur wheat
450 ml/16 fl oz boiling water
1 tsp sea salt
$\frac{1}{2}$ tsp ground allspice
1 red onion, diced
225 g/8 oz fresh curly or flat-leaf
   parsley, chopped
$\frac{1}{2}$ medium cucumber, seeded,
   peeled and diced
3 spring onions, thinly sliced
100 g/3 oz mint leaves, chopped
3 Tbsp fresh lemon juice
3 Tbsp olive oil

Put the bulghur wheat in a heatproof bowl. Pour over the boiling water. Leave the bulghur to stand for 1 hour. In a large bowl stir together the red onion, salt and allspice and leave to stand for 30 minutes. Drain the bulghur in a sieve, pressing hard to remove the excess water. Combine the drained bulghur, parsley, cucumber, spring onions and mint. Combine the lemon juice and oil and blend well. Pour over the bulghur mixture and toss. Cover and chill.

SMOKED POTATO SALAD

Serves 6 to 8

900 g/2 lb small red potatoes
1 Tbsp sea salt
3 Tbsp soya oil
8 to 10 rashers bacon
6 spring onions, thinly sliced
2 Tbsp cider vinegar
3 Tbsp soya oil
1 clove garlic, crushed
1 tsp sea salt
$\frac{1}{2}$ tsp white pepper

Rinse the potatoes of any dirt, place in a stockpot and cover with cold water by 5 centimetres/2 inches. Bring to the boil. Add the salt and simmer, covered, until the potatoes are just tender, 10 to 15 minutes. Drain in a colander and cool.

Cut the potatoes in half, place in a bowl and pour over 3 tablespoons oil. Toss to coat. Place in a smoker and smoke for 15 minutes to 1 hour, depending on the amount of smoke that you want and the smoking equipment you have.

Fry the bacon until crisp, reserving 2 tablespoons of the dripping, and drain on kitchen paper. Crumble or dice the bacon.

In a large bowl toss the potatoes with reserved dripping, bacon, spring onions, vinegar, remaining oil, garlic, salt and pepper.

Tabbouleh

RISOTTO WITH PANCETTA AND WILD MUSHROOMS

Serves 6 to 8

8 to 12 paper-thin slices pancetta
   or lean bacon
2 Tbsp extra-virgin olive oil
15 g/½ oz unsalted butter
450 g/1 lb mixed mushrooms,
   chanterelles, oyster and shiitake,
   thickly sliced
2 tsp sea salt
40 g/1½ oz unsalted butter
1 tsp fresh tarragon leaves,
   chopped
1.1 l/2 pt chicken stock
2 cloves garlic, crushed
3 shallots, diced
300 g/10 oz arborio rice
125 g/4 oz grated Parmesan
2 Tbsp whipping cream
1 tsp sea salt
1 tsp freshly ground white pepper
50 g/2 oz shaved Parmesan cheese

Grill or bake the pancetta or bacon until crisp, drain on kitchen paper then crumble. In a large non-stick frying pan over medium-high heat add the olive oil and 15 g/½ oz butter. Add the mushrooms, season with salt and sauté over high heat until the mushrooms exude their juice, 3 to 5 minutes. Transfer the mushrooms and their liquid to a strainer, set over a bowl and press lightly on the mushrooms; reserve the liquid. Add 15 g/½ oz butter to a clean frying pan over medium heat and sauté, stirring, until tender and just beginning to brown, 2 to 3 minutes. Add the tarragon and set aside.

In a medium saucepan, combine the stock and mushroom liquid, bring to a simmer and keep warm over low heat. Melt 15 g/½ oz butter in a deep non-stick frying pan. Add the garlic and sauté until just fragrant. Add the shallots and cook until soft but not browned, 3 to 4 minutes. Add the rice and stir until the grains are coated with butter. Add 225 ml/8 fl oz of stock and cook, stirring constantly, until the stock is absorbed, 1 to 2 minutes. Continue to cook the risotto, adding 225 ml/8 fl oz stock at a time, stirring constantly between additions, until it is absorbed. Cook until creamy, about 20 minutes. Remove from the heat and stir in the Parmesan, cream and remaining butter. Season with salt and pepper and transfer to a serving bowl. Garnish with pancetta, mushrooms and shavings of Parmesan cheese. Serve immediately.

GLAZED SWEET POTATOES

Serves 4 to 6

4 medium sweet potatoes
225 g/8 oz brown sugar
125 g/4 oz butter
About 1 l/1¾ pt water
1 tsp sea salt

Peel the potatoes and cut into 5-centimetre/2-inch slices or chunks. Put the cut potatoes in a wide, heavy frying pan. Add water to a quarter of the way up the sides of the frying pan, cover and cook slowly until they can be pierced with a fork. Remove from the heat and drain the water from the pan. Sprinkle the sugar over the potatoes, add butter and salt, and return to low heat. Cook, uncovered, until the liquid is sticky.

Wheat Berry Waldorf Salad

Serves 6 to 8

125 g/4 oz wheat berries (whole-
   grain, hard wheat)
1 l/1³/₄ pt water
1 tsp sea salt
1 McIntosh apple, diced
1 Granny Smith apple, diced
1 l/1³/₄ pt water mixed with 2 Tbsp
   lemon juice
1 small stalk celery, diced
50 g/2 oz dried sour cherries
50 g/2 oz sultanas
3 Tbsp chopped fresh mint
4 spring onions, thinly sliced
3 Tbsp seasoned rice wine vinegar
3 Tbsp fresh orange juice
1 tsp grated orange rind
1 tsp sea salt
¹/₂ tsp white pepper
2 Tbsp walnuts, roasted and chopped

In a saucepan bring the water and salt to the boil and add the wheat berries. Reduce the heat and simmer, covered, for 1¹/₂ hours or until tender. Drain the wheat berries in a colander and cool to room temperature. Place the apples in the lemon water and set aside. Combine the celery, cherries, sultanas, mint and spring onions in a large bowl. In another bowl combine the vinegar, orange juice and orange rind. Drain the apples and add them to the celery mixture. Add the cooled wheat berries. Pour the orange juice mixture over the wheat berries and toss until well blended. Season with salt and pepper and garnish with roasted walnuts.

HARICOT BEAN AND RED ONION SALAD

Serves 8 to 10

400 g/14 oz dried haricot beans
1 Tbsp coarsely ground coriander
2 bay leaves
2 tsp freshly ground black pepper

FOR THE DRESSING

4 cloves garlic, crushed
3 Tbsp fresh lemon juice
125 ml/4 fl oz olive oil
2 tsp sea salt
2 red onions, diced
3 Tbsp chopped fresh coriander
3 Tbsp chopped fresh parsley

Rinse the beans with cold water. Add the beans to a stockpot with the ground coriander, bay leaves and black pepper. Cover with cold water about 5 centimetres/2 inches above. Simmer the beans, stirring occasionally. If necessary, add hot water as the cooking proceeds to keep the beans covered. Simmer for 1 to 1½ hours or until beans are tender but not mushy.

Combine the garlic and lemon juice and beat in the olive oil with a wire whisk, until well blended.

Drain the beans in a colander and discard the bay leaves. Add the beans to a large bowl and pour over the dressing. Toss and season with salt. Leave the salad to cool then stir in the onions, coriander and parsley.

BROCCOLI, BACON AND ONION SALAD

Serves 6 to 8

10 to 12 rashers bacon
150 ml/5 fl oz olive oil
3 Tbsp red wine vinegar
1 red onion, diced
375 g/12 oz broccoli florets,
    blanched and chilled
125 g/4 oz raisins, soaked in hot
    water and chilled
50 g/2 oz sunflower seeds, roasted
1 tsp granulated sugar
1 tsp sea salt
1 tsp coarse ground black pepper

Fry the bacon until crisp and drain on kitchen paper. Whisk the oil and vinegar in a medium bowl to blend. Mix in the onions. Combine the broccoli, raisins and sunflower seeds and gently toss to blend. Season with sugar, salt and pepper. Pour the dressing over the salad and toss to coat evenly. Crumble the bacon over the top of the salad and serve.

Haricot Bean and Red Onion Salad

HONEY RED CABBAGE

Serves 6 to 8

3 Tbsp sunflower oil
1 large onion, thinly sliced
3 large cloves garlic, crushed
1 medium red cabbage, shredded
   and chopped
2 Granny Smith apples, quartered,
   cored and thinly sliced
2 Tbsp white wine vinegar
1 Tbsp granulated sugar
2 Tbsp fresh dill
3 Tbsp clear honey
1 tsp sea salt
1 tsp freshly ground black pepper

Heat the oil in a large frying pan. Add the onions and sauté until soft, about 3 to 4 minutes. Add the garlic and cook for a further minute. Stir in the cabbage and cook, covered, for about 4 minutes or until the cabbage has wilted. Add the apples, vinegar, sugar and dill. Stir well and continue to cook until the apples are tender, 7 to 8 minutes. Stir in honey, season with salt and pepper and cook for a further 2 minutes.

BUTTERMILK COLESLAW

Serves 6 to 8

1 medium green cabbage, shredded
   and chopped
2 medium onions, diced
1 large green pepper, diced
1 large red pepper, diced
1 large stalk celery, thinly sliced
50 g/2 oz grated carrots
225 ml/8 fl oz buttermilk
125 ml/4 fl oz mayonnaise
1 tsp celery seeds
1 tsp sea salt
1/2 tsp white pepper

Combine the cabbage, onion, green pepper, red pepper, celery and carrot in a large bowl and gently toss. In another bowl add the buttermilk, mayonnaise, celery seeds, salt and pepper and blend well with a wire whisk. Pour over the cabbage mixture and blend well. Cover and chill. Serve cold.

Honey Red Cabbage

Smoked Corn on the Cob with Flavoured Butters

Serves 4 to 8

8 large fresh corn on the cob, with husk and silk left intact
3.6 l/6½ pt water
225 g/8 oz butter or flavoured butters
Salt and pepper to taste

Cut any corn silk sticking out of the top of the ear. Place the corn cobs in a large bucket and pour over water. Weigh the cobs down with a weighted plate, keeping them submerged. Soak the corn for at least 8 hours, longer if possible. To cook place in a smoke-roaster and cook for at least 2 hours. It is difficult to overcook the corn because the wet husk protects it. To serve, peel or shuck the corn and smear with plain or flavoured butter, salt and pepper to taste.

Sun-dried tomato butter

125 g/4 oz unsalted butter, softened
1 clove garlic, crushed
2 tsp fresh lemon juice
½ tsp sea salt
2 Tbsp sun-dried tomatoes in oil, drained and finely minced
3 Tbsp chopped coriander
1 plum tomato, peeled, seeded and chopped

Place the butter, garlic, lemon juice, salt, sun-dried tomatoes, coriander and fresh tomato in a small bowl, and beat until well blended. Place in a small serving bowl. Serve at room temperature.

Chilli-avocado butter

2 Tbsp fresh lime juice
2 Tbsp water
1 small ripe avocado, peeled, stoned and chopped
125 g/4 oz unsalted butter, softened
1 small ancho or other mild dried chilli, stemmed and seeded
1 tsp grated lime rind
1 tsp sea salt
½ tsp white pepper

Combine the lime juice and water in a small bowl. Add the diced avocado to the lime water. In another small bowl combine the butter, chilli, lime rind, salt and pepper and blend well. Add the avocado and blend in until incorporated. Place in a small bowl. Serve the butter at room temperature.

Mixed herb butter

125 g/4 oz unsalted butter, softened
2 Tbsp chopped fresh flat-leaf parsley
2 Tbsp chopped fresh watercress leaves
1 Tbsp chopped fresh mint leaves
1 Tbsp freshly grated Parmesan
1 tsp fresh tarragon leaves, chopped
1 tsp Pernod
1 tsp grated lemon rind
1/2 tsp hot chilli sauce
1/2 tsp sea salt
1/4 tsp white pepper

Place the butter, parsley, watercress, mint, Parmesan, tarragon, Pernod, lemon rind, hot sauce, salt and pepper in a small bowl, and beat until well blended. Serve at room temperature.

CUCUMBER AND DILL SALAD

Serves 6 to 8

4 medium cucumbers, peeled and thinly sliced
Juice of 2 lemons
1 tsp sea salt
1 cup soured cream
6 spring onions, thinly sliced
1/2 tsp white pepper
2 tsp fresh dill
1 tsp granulated sugar

Place the cucumbers in a non-reactive bowl, squeeze over the lemon juice with 1/2 teaspoon salt and gently toss. Cover and chill in the refrigerator for 30 minutes. Blend the soured cream, onions, remaining salt, pepper and dill in a small bowl. Drain the cucumbers in a colander. Put the cucumbers back in the bowl. Fold the soured cream mixture into the cucumbers. Taste and adjust the seasoning with salt, pepper, lemon juice and sugar.

SOUTHERN CORNBREAD

Serves 8

3 Tbsp bacon dripping
175 g/6 oz cornmeal
50 g/2 oz self-raising flour
1 large egg
225 ml/8 fl oz full-cream milk

Pre-heat the oven to 260°C/500°F/Gas Mark 10. Pour the bacon dripping into a 23-centimetre/9-inch cast-iron frying pan or a 23-centimetre/9-inch square baking tin and heat in the oven for 3 to 4 minutes.

Mix the cornmeal, flour, egg and milk in a small bowl with a wire whisk or a fork. Remove the frying pan from the oven and blend half the dripping into the cornmeal mixture. Pour into the hot tin and bake for 15 minutes. Cut into wedges or squares to serve.

SOUTHERN CORNSTICKS

Makes 16

150 ml/5 fl oz sunflower oil
125 g/4 oz cornmeal
225 ml/8 fl oz buttermilk
1 large egg
2 Tbsp sunflower oil
1 tsp sea salt

Pre-heat the oven to 260°C/500°F/Gas Mark 10. Put 1½ teaspoons of oil in each of the 8 sections of 2 cornstick tins, or 3 teaspoons in each of 8 large bun tins. Use a pastry brush to coat each entire section with oil. Place the tins in the oven until they are very hot. Combine the cornmeal, buttermilk, egg, oil and salt in a small mixing bowl. Mix with a wire whisk or a fork. The mixture will be runny. Remove the hot tins from the oven and fill each section half-full with the cornmeal mixture. Bake the cornsticks for 20 minutes.

HOE CAKES

Makes 8 to 12

White vegetable fat
125 g/4 oz cornmeal
1 tsp sea salt
225 ml/8 fl oz boiling water

Heat about 5 millimetres/¼ inch white vegetable fat in a heavy 23- or 25-centimetre/9- or 10-inch frying pan (cast iron is best), until it is almost smoking. While the oil is heating, mix the cornmeal and salt in a bowl. Beat in the boiling water with a spoon until you achieve a thick consistency. Drop from the spoon into the fat and fry until golden on the bottom. Turn and fry the other side. Drain on kitchen paper.

Southern Cornbread

ARTICHOKE AND PASTA SALAD

Serves 6

One 400-g/14-oz tin artichoke hearts, drained and divided
1 Tbsp olive oil
1 Tbsp water
1 Tbsp fresh lemon juice
¹/₂ tsp dried basil
¹/₄ tsp dried oregano
¹/₄ tsp black pepper
1 clove garlic, chopped
375 g/12 oz cooked radiatori or other pasta shapes
50 g/2 oz spinach, thinly sliced
4 plum tomatoes, seeded and chopped
Basil leaves, to garnish
50 g/2 oz crumbled feta cheese

Combine two of the artichoke hearts with the olive oil, water, lemon juice, basil, oregano, black pepper and garlic in a blender or food processor fitted with a steel blade and process until smooth.

Coarsely chop the remaining artichoke hearts and combine with the pasta, spinach and chopped tomato in a large bowl. Pour the puréed artichoke mixture over the pasta mixture and toss well to coat.

Cover and chill for 2 hours. Sprinkle with basil leaves and feta cheese to serve.

Artichoke and Pasta Salad

RED BEAN AND RICE SALAD

Serves 8 to 10

375 g/12 oz cooked small red beans
50 g/2 oz cooked long-grain rice
2 stalks celery, thinly sliced, with leaves
1 medium onion, diced
4 plum tomatoes, seeded and diced
1 small green pepper, seeded and diced
4 cloves garlic, crushed

FOR THE DRESSING

5 Tbsp bottled Italian salad dressing
2 Tbsp water
2 Tbsp white vinegar
1 tsp sea salt
$\frac{1}{2}$ tsp freshly ground black pepper
$\frac{1}{2}$ tsp fresh oregano leaves
$\frac{1}{2}$ tsp cayenne
$\frac{1}{4}$ tsp fresh thyme leaves

Combine the red beans, rice, celery, onions, tomatoes, green pepper and garlic in a large bowl and blend gently. In another bowl combine the dressing, water, vinegar, salt, pepper, oregano, cayenne and thyme and mix well. Pour the dressing over the red bean mixture and toss gently to coat. Cover and chill for about 1 hour to allow the flavours to develop.

PICKLED CABBAGE

Serves 6 to 8

5 Tbsp sea salt or pickling salt
300 ml/10 fl oz boiling water
12 banana peppers, stemmed,
   seeded and cored
225 g/8 oz granulated sugar
3 Tbsp white vinegar
3 Tbsp cold water
½ tsp sea salt
700 g/1½ lb shredded green
   cabbage
300 ml/10 fl oz water
100 ml/4 fl oz white vinegar
1 to 3 tsp hot red pepper flakes
1 Tbsp grated lemon rind
½ tsp sea salt
½ tsp freshly ground black pepper
   or white pepper

This recipe needs some forethought since it should stand for 2 to 3 days. In a medium heatproof bowl, combine 5 tablespoons salt with the boiling water, dissolving the salt. Leave to cool. Add the peppers to the brine and cover with a plate to keep them submerged. Leave to stand overnight at room temperature. In a large bowl, combine 125 g/4 oz sugar, 3 tablespoons vinegar, 3 tablespoons cold water and ½ teaspoon salt. Add the shredded cabbage and toss to coat evenly, cover and leave to stand for 45 minutes.

Drain the cabbage and peppers, discarding the pickle and brine. Thinly slice the peppers crossways.

Add the remaining sugar, water, vinegar, hot red pepper flakes, lemon rind, salt and pepper to a large saucepan. Bring to the boil, stirring constantly until a syrup forms, about 3 to 4 minutes. Add the cabbage and peppers and cook for 2 to 3 minutes. If you want a sharp pickle add more vinegar to taste. Pack in pickle jars or a large sealing bowl and refrigerate for 2 to 3 days before serving.

SUNFLOWER SLAW

Serves 6 to 8

50 g/2 oz sunflower seeds
50 g/2 oz sliced almonds
50 g/2 oz Ramen noodles
100 ml/4 fl oz seasoned rice vinegar
225 g/8 oz granulated sugar
1 Tbsp soy sauce
100 to 225 ml/4 to 8 fl oz
   sunflower oil
1 large Chinese cabbage, shredded
6 spring onions, thinly sliced
1 red pepper, shredded

Place the sunflower seeds on a baking sheet and roast. Place the almonds on another baking sheet and roast until golden brown, taking care not to burn. Crumble the Ramen noodles onto a baking sheet and roast until just browned. Combine in a bowl and reserve.

Combine the rice vinegar, sugar and soy sauce and heat to dissolve the sugar. Allow to cool. When cool combine the oil and vinegar mixture with a wire whisk.

In a large serving bowl combine the cabbage, onions and peppers and toss to blend. Cover and chill.

Do not assemble the salad until you are ready to serve it. To serve, pour the cooled dressing over the slaw, sprinkle the roasted mixture over the salad and toss well.

Green Bean and New Potato Salad

Serves 10 to 12

900 g/2 lb new potatoes, scrubbed
    and rinsed
1 Tbsp sea salt
450 g/1 lb fresh green beans,
    trimmed
1 Tbsp sea salt
3 Tbsp chopped mint
3 Tbsp chopped chives
2 Tbsp chopped fresh parsley
1 Tbsp chopped fresh thyme
3 Tbsp extra-virgin olive oil
Juice of 1 lemon
1 Tbsp grated lemon rind
1 tsp sea salt
1 tsp freshly ground black pepper

Add the potatoes to a large stockpot with 1 tablespoon salt and cover by 5 centimetres/2 inches with water. Cook, covered, for 10 to 15 minutes or until the potatoes are just tender. Place 1 l/1³/₄ pints water and 1 tablespoon salt in another stockpot and bring to the boil. Add the green beans, cover and cook until tender but still crisp, 4 to 5 minutes. Drain the potatoes and beans in a colander. Place in a large bowl. In a small bowl combine the mint, chives, parsley, thyme, oil, lemon rind, salt and pepper and blend well. Pour over the warm potato and bean mixture and gently toss, coating well. Chill or serve warm.

PECAN PIE

Serves 8 to 10

125 ml/4 fl oz treacle
225 g/8 oz granulated sugar
50 g/2 oz butter, melted
3 large eggs, beaten to bright yellow
175 g/6 oz pecan halves
One 23-cm/9-in unbaked shortcrust
   pastry shell

Pre-heat the oven to 200°C/400°F/Gas Mark 6.

In a medium mixing bowl, combine the treacle, sugar and butter and mix well. Add the eggs and pecans and blend in. Fill the unbaked pastry shell with the mixture. Bake for 10 minutes in the middle of the oven. Reduce the heat to 175°C/350°F/Gas Mark 4 and continue baking for 30 to 35 minutes, until set around the edges. The pie will not be completely set in the middle when done. Cool before serving.

PECAN BISCUITS WITH PEACHES AND CREAM

Serves 10 to 15

175 g/6 oz pecans
175 g/6 oz butter
6 Tbsp granulated sugar
175 g/6 oz flour
$^1/_2$ tsp sea salt
Icing sugar (optional)

FOR THE FILLING

225 ml/8 fl oz double cream,
   whipped
1 tsp vanilla essence
2 tsp granulated sugar
3 to 4 medium fresh ripe peaches or
   other fruit in season, sliced
Additional whipped cream (optional)
Icing sugar (optional)

Pre-heat the oven to 190°C/375°F/Gas Mark 5.

Brown the nuts in the oven for 5 to 10 minutes, taking care they do not burn. Cool then chop them in a grater or food processor until they are fine, but not a powder. Cream the butter and sugar together. Sift the flour with the salt, add the nuts, and stir into the creamed mixture to make a smooth dough. Divide into 3 equal pieces and shape into flat rounds. Place each between 2 sheets of greaseproof paper and chill for 30 minutes or until firm. Roll or pat out into 3-millimetre/$^1/_8$-inch thick rounds. Refrigerate if hard to handle. Remove the top layer of paper and cut into small 5 or 8-centimetre/2 or 3-inch rounds with a biscuit cutter. Bake on a baking sheet for 10 minutes or until the edges begin to brown. Be careful not to overbake. They will be soft when cooked and will harden as they cool. Remove them from the baking sheet to a cooling rack. Cool.

Store, covered, at room temperature or in a freezer. One hour before serving, whip the cream with vanilla and sugar. Sandwich the whipped cream and peaches between two biscuits. Immediately before serving, decorate the top with additional whipped cream and/or sprinkle with icing sugar.